The Morning Hill Solar Cookery Bool techniques, and tips of all kinds for solar matter what kind of cooker you have, you will be able to use the recipes in this book to produce hearty, healthy vegetarian food which will please all tastes.

from the author:

I grew up in Vermont, where I first learned to cook from my mother when I was 8 or 9 years old. I was always creative — my mother teased me about the famous "rubber cake" I made the first time I tried to create a recipe. As a child, I had a dreamed of owning a ski lodge, where the happy, healthy guests would gather around the table in the evening for a home-cooked feast. I equated good food with happiness, and indeed, if health contributes to happiness, then good food has quite a lot to do with it too!

As an adult, I noticed that when I was eating whole foods, I did not have a problem with my weight or energy level. At age 37, I finally realized my dream of a ski lodge by building Garrison Springs Lodge, a small backcountry ski lodge. I catered successfully to the demand for vegetarian food, and gained a reputation for creative, delicious, healthy cooking. When I met Lance, he convinced me to give up the last processed and refined foods I was using and a whole new world of healthy cooking opened up to me.

When I closed the lodge and moved to Oregon to marry Lance, I was able to pour my creative energy into the shaping of my own style of wholefoods cookery. I did a lot of research which further convinced me that the healthiest foods were those that were closest to the way nature made them. I began teaching wholefoods cooking classes at Blue Mountain Community College Extension, and tested my newly-developed recipes on my enthusiastic students. The recipes developed during this time turned into **The Morning Hill Cookbook**.

Meanwhile, living in a solar-powered house, my husband and I were having fun and educating ourselves about renewable energy by attending solar fairs. At a fair in Willits, California, I saw Joseph Radabaugh simmering beans in a cooker made from a cardboard box. I bought the plans for his SunStar cooker from him, and after an afternoon of cutting, pasting, and gluing foil, I too was cooking with the sun. As soon as **The Morning Hill Cookbook** was off the press, I was creating fresh recipes to go with my new way of cooking. The next Christmas, Lance gave me a commercial cooker with shiny reflectors. The possibilities exploded. The sun draws out the creativity in me! I can't stop creating new recipes! I hope you like the results.

.....*Jennifer Stein Barker, March 21st, 1999*

The Morning Hill
Solar Cookery Book

By Jennifer Stein Barker

Illustrated by Joy Lane

Morning Hill Associates
15013 Geary Creek Road
Canyon City, OR 97820
541-542-2525

SECOND PRINTING, July 2008

Printed on recycled paper. This book was typeset in Arial on Microsoft Works.
The computer was powered entirely by solar power.

Library of Congress # 99-70204

ISBN 0-9642977-1-X

Table of Contents

This book is dedicated: To Mom, who liked to come and visit us, and putter in our garden, because we "took after" her.

To Lance, my sweetie as always, for his patience and support.

To Joe Radabaugh and Kathleen Jarschke-Schultze, whose never-flagging enthusiasm for solar cooking has inspired me to new heights of creativity.

Thanks also to Heather Sheedy who proofread my book as well as the local newspaper; to Joy Lane, whose folksy drawings adorn the pages; to David Judson for the computer help; to Bill and Linda Hutchinson whose friendly local print shop produced the copy you are reading; to the Seneca collating crew; and to all the others who gave me help and advice.

INTRODUCTION

WHAT IS MORNING HILL?

Morning Hill is the place where we are learning to live in harmony with our environment. It's the first place in our neighborhood the sun touches on rising each morning. We live in a 600-square-foot house surrounded by 40 acres of second-growth Ponderosa Pine. The house is entirely powered by the sun through photovoltaic panels. An inverter provides AC current for conveniences like a freezer, computer, and stereo. We don't have any generator or grid power here, and we never have. When the sun doesn't shine for weeks at a time, we plan out our power usage much as one would plan to use scarce time when a person is busy. We don't regard this as a hardship, but rather as an opportunity to learn to live with what is given.

We farm a three-acre organic garden for as much of our food as we can grow in our climate, where the official season between occurrences of 32 degrees is 16 days. It is difficult to farm here, but Lance has through perseverance and inventiveness learned to grow root vegetables, greens, alliums (garlic and onion family), cabbage family, peas, and berry fruits very well. We rarely miss the tender foods we can't grow. We have so much good, healthy food from our garden that we cannot eat it all! If you notice there are few recipes in this book that call for the likes of corn and green beans, it is because we rarely have them.

We work for a paycheck sometimes, to buy what we need, but our goal is this: to do for ourselves as much as we can; to use the nonrenewable natural resources of the earth as lightly as possible; to restore the renewable resources of our land (watershed, native vegetation, and wildlife habitat); to live as healthy lives as we can; and to provide example, encouragement, and support for others who wish to live healthy lives in harmony with the earth.

WHY SOLAR COOKING?

Solar cooking is another way of using the resource of the sun which is freely given. Any container with reflectors to collect solar heat can serve as a cooker, but there are several designs which work efficiently enough to make cooking with the sun a practical daily alternative. Cooking with the sun is a way of making a statement on how we feel about our earth and its resources. It is a way of saving the time and money we would otherwise spend to obtain energy for cooking with electricity, wood, or fossil fuels. It is a way of stating our independence from "the system" which runs the energy supply infrastructure. And it is a way of making carefree time coincide with the creation of delicious food.

You can't hurry the sun. Some days are jewels, with azure blue skies and blazing white sun. Others, soft pastels of pale sky and daffodil sunshine, take longer to cook a meal or fully charge the solar power system in our house. Yet more days are in-and-out, peekaboo blue sky and solar shadows on the earth. We have to look at the sky each day and judge for ourselves what will work for us and our food. Ultimately, the only rule is **cook it till it's done**. Experience will tell us when that is possible.

DIFFERENT DESIGNS FOR SOLAR COOKERS

This is not a manual on how to build solar cookers, but a brief explanation of some different designs is called for here. Bigger is often better in the world of solar cookers. Tom Burns' "Villager" stands taller than a tall person, needs a trailer to be moved around, and can bake 50 loaves of bread in an hour. I have tried some of the small, portable cookers on the other end of the spectrum, and they cook slowly enough that it would take two or three of them to cook enough food for my husband and myself. They are handy for traveling, or where space or weight is an issue, but my working tools fall somewhere between the smallest and largest.

The number and design of the reflectors also has a great deal to do with efficiency. Box-type cookers are a flat box with glass in the top, and a single reflector that props up on a stick. More efficient than these are the multiple-reflector cookers, which have four or more reflectors and are tilted to compensate for sun angle. The most efficient cookers are parabolic cookers which focus the sun's rays on a single point, concentrating the heat to obtain temperatures as high as a regular stovetop. For a complete discussion of types of solar cookers including instructions on how to build them, and for tips and techniques different than my own, you should read Joe Radabaugh's **Heaven's Flame, a Guide to Solar Cookers**. To obtain it, see the **Sources** section in the back of this book (p.97).

All my work for this cookbook has been done with multiple-reflector cookers, which provide the most familiar oven-like box and temperatures. They are easy to focus on the sun, and provide relatively carefree cooking because they have a wide angle of sun acceptance. The ones I have used will maintain near-optimum heat for up to an hour on a single focusing. This allows the cooking of many types of foods with minimum attention. What a joy it is to set food to cook in the sun, then spend my time working in the garden or relaxing in the shade!

A PHILOSOPHY OF COOKING

Don't put any more time into it than it's worth. If you wish to prepare an elegant meal, and you love to cook, by all means spend several hours serving up a feast as a declaration of love, creativity or whatever you wish to express through food. But if spending time in the kitchen isn't at the top of your list (this world needs many, many things from you besides your good cooking), don't give up any more time than you can spare to the preparation of food. Nutrition and enjoyment in eating should be of more importance than complexity of preparation, and these may be found in the simplest meal, if it is made of fresh and high-quality food.

A PHILOSOPHY OF EATING

If the eating of food were only to sustain life, we could eat a bowl of steamed grain three times a day (as many people in impoverished nations do), and we would stay alive. But food is also a building block for **optimum** health, and often the center of our social events. If our food is varied and of the best quality (this means organically grown), we are much more likely to get all of the nutrition we need. We can spread the word about how wonderful truly good food is. If our food is also chosen with attention to its impact on the environment, we can make the choice to move the earth towards a healthier future for us as well as all its other inhabitants.

A HOMEMADE BOOK

This book is an entirely community-made product. The text was produced at home on a solar-powered laptop computer. Illustrations were done by Joy Lane, whose talents we discovered when she participated in the collating party for the Morning Hill Cookbook. Offset printing was done at Hutch's printing in John Day, and the collating was done by an enthusiastic crew of community members in Seneca (pop. 230).

The way we produced the book keeps all the proceeds of the sale in our community. We looked around our small county (pop. 8,000) and found we had all the talent we needed to produce a book from start to finish. We would encourage anyone who wants to try a similar project to do the same.

Jennifer Stein Barker
Morning Hill Forest Farm
January 25, 1999

IX

Lance and Jennifer's sunny eastern Oregon home
with two of Jennifer's solar cookers in the foreground.

X

The Solar Meal

Main Dishes
Casseroles
Soups
Stews
The Basics

"THAT'S TOO MUCH WORK"

A while ago I wrote that the neighbors looked at our woodpiles made of small pieces and said "that's too much work." In fact, we hear that statement about a lot of the things we do. People also think that raising an extensive garden organically is "too much work." Ditto cooking on a woodstove, excavating for our new shop by hand with a shovel, and many, many other things we choose to do. We are getting the distinct impression that physical work is not only no longer valued, but looked down on in our society.

Used to be that a person who knew the value of hand work was respected and even admired. The more different skills a person could number to their account, and the more facets of their life they could provide for by their own labor, the better off they were considered to be. However, today what is valued seems to be the ability to work at a high-paying job in order to buy machines and the services of others to perform the labor for you. Physical work is associated with suffering and deprivation. Ironically, many of the people who feel this way can be seen jogging and "working out" to stay in shape, because they don't get enough physical activity.

The things we do which our acquaintances call "too much work" allow us to have a high quality of life without being rich. In fact, we get things that way that money just can't pay for. We get our firewood without having to own and maintain an expensive vehicle to haul it, and improve the quality of our landscape to a park-like serenity at the same time. Gardening organically improves our soil instead of depleting it, and also provides us with fresher, more nutritious food than money can buy. When people eat bread or cakes fresh from my woodstove, they say "Oh! How wonderful! You can't get crusty, moist bread like this any more...but, it's so much work (they almost sigh)."

By doing his shop excavation by hand, Lance was able to carefully separate the best native topsoil on our land as he dug it, and cart it off to a large depression in our garden that needed to be filled. Instead of being lost in a big heap piled up by a backhoe, that wonderful ash and organic topsoil is now the most productive part of our potato bed. The back of the hole from which it was removed is being turned into a root-cellar to store the bounty (last year we harvested 300 pounds of potatoes). Another benefit, possibly no less important, was the learning experience of closely observing the geological history in the layers. Lance saved a jar of chunks of ash from the eruption of Mt. Mazama that created Crater Lake about 5,000 years ago.

Not everyone follows the majority opinion, of course. In some measure, we choose our friends by noticing who among them discerns that, rather than suffering by our physical labors, we are the possessors of a quality of life that money can't buy. Those people look at our glowingly healthy pine woods, our warm and cozy house, and our bountiful table, and they repeat "you folks aren't suffering **at all**!" And they say it with respect for the thoughtful, mindful, physical hand-work which has gone into the production of this life.

....from the "Morning Hill News" #25, September/October '95

2

WELCOME to the world of solar cookery! Your solar cooker is your path to lots of fun and delicious food, all without using purchased energy. You won't have to heat up your house in order to bake in the summertime. Just set your food to cook in the sun, and go off to work in the garden!

TIPS AND ADVICE: This book is full of handy tips and general advice for cooking in your solar cooker. The recipes are created for use with wholegrains and natural foods, available from your local co-op or health food store. All the recipes are vegetarian, though meat may be added to any of the casseroles as you wish. Let's start with some of the most general advice:

COOK IT TILL IT'S DONE: This is the most important "rule of thumb" with a solar cooker. The sun varies in intensity by location and weather. A fully sunny blue-sky day will provide more intense cooking heat than a hazy day . Some partly-cloudy days will cook just fine, but slower. Casseroles will do better on partly-cloudy days than baked goods, because length of cooking time affects the quality of a casserole less. Experience will tell you what works best in your area, with your cooker.

KEEP IT CLEAN: Always keep your solar cooker clean! Wipe any spills out of the cooker's interior immediately after use, so they don't have a chance to cook on. Clean the glass with soap and water. Use your softest, cleanest rags to polish the reflectors, taking care not to scratch them. Clean reflectors heat best.

FOOD SAFETY. Food should be kept below 45 degrees or above 140 degrees. It should not spend more than four hours in between those temperatures in the heating or cooling process. Meats, beans, and eggs are the most likely foods to develop hazardous bacteria. If you do not have full sun to heat your food quickly and thoroughly, please try to avoid these foods!

GENERAL INSTRUCTIONS. Any food that splatters should be well contained to keep your cooker clean. Always cover a casserole to keep as much steam inside the dish as you can. A steamed-up glass seems to transmit plenty of sunlight, but it is harder to see if your cooker is facing the sun perfectly if you can't see the shadows inside. When the food is done, you may close the reflectors over the glass to keep it warm a short time until needed. **Always use oven mitts or hotpads** when approaching your solar cooker! Many consider it to be a good idea to use sunglasses, too. It is **hot** and **bright** in the vicinity.

POTS AND PANS: Dark pans and casseroles absorb more heat and help food cook more quickly. My favorite casserole dish is a 2-liter covered amber glass casserole. The darker color absorbs heat well, and you can see through the lid to watch the progress of cooking food. Other good choices are granite-ware pots (but you can't see into them without opening your cooker) and clear glass casseroles (but they are a little slower). If you are using an opaque metal pot, it helps to attach a magnetic woodstove thermometer to the side of the pot where it will be visible.

HOW MUCH TO COOK: A 2-liter casserole will feed four normal people if there is also bread, salad, and dessert. You can use a bigger casserole, but the more you put into a solar cooker at one time, the slower it will reach cooking temperatures, until you reach the point of inefficiency. Experience will tell you what that point is in your area, with your family's needs to consider.

BOILING WATER: Use a wide-mouth jar painted black to boil water (use tape to mask off a stripe before painting so contents can be viewed during cooking). If you don't like handling hot glass with boiling water in it (I don't), a granite ware teakettle with a wire handle makes a great water vessel. If you like the jar method, it can be used to cook all sorts of beans and grains, as well as plain water. Several jars may fit in your cooker together, for a multi-dish meal.

☼

PREHEATING: It is perfectly OK to close the Sun Oven door when pre-heating. If you live at high altitude (as the author does), and the air is extremely clear, you should check occasionally to make sure the Sun Oven is not getting too hot (over 425 degrees). A small container of water in the cooker will keep it from overheating, since the mass of the water will not get hotter than 212º. Preheating will be necessary when you do bread, cakes, and other risen foods, but is not necessary for casseroles.

WATCHING THE SUN: Find a spot to put your solar cooker where there is unobstructed sun access. At 2 p.m. on a sunny day, go out and move around until your shadow falls on your cooker. Put a marker at your feet. It's handy to know what direction to aim your solar cooker for mid-afternoon cooking. Familiarize yourself with the sun's travel path.

TIMING OF MULTIPLE DISHES: Got a lot of things to cook in one day? Experience will show you when the earliest practical time is that the sun is high enough to get your cooker hot in your area. At my house, that's around 8:45 a.m. in midsummer. If you have the next dish ready to go when the last one comes out of the cooker, you can get several things baked in one day. Here's a sample timeline illustrating the dance of keeping food ready:

8:45 a.m.: **Fresh Apple Bread** (p.62) in cooker. Baking time 1:10. Mix and knead **Rustic Bread** (p.73) while the apple bread bakes. Set bread to rise.
9:45 a.m.: Prepare **Bulgur With Greens and Cheese** (p.6).
10:00 a.m.: **Fresh Apple bread** is done. **Bulgur With Greens and Cheese** in cooker. Baking time 1:50.
11:15 a.m.: Shape **Rustic Bread** into loaf and set to rise.
12:00 p.m.: **Rustic Bread** in cooker. Baking time 1:20. Stir the greens into the **Bulgur With Greens and Cheese** and eat!
1:30 p.m.: melt chocolate for the **Chocolate-mint Ricotta Mousse** (p.54). Baking time 15 minutes.
2:00 p.m.: Put the evening's casserole in the cooker, either **Curried Rice and Lentils** (p. 10) or **Mama Gianna's Easy Vegie Lasagna** (p.14). Baking time 3:30.
6:00 p.m.: The casserole should be done by now, and the sun is dropping below the trees. If you aren't ready to eat, close the reflectors over the cooker to keep dinner warm.

(Note that this is a midsummer day! If you want to cook this much on a shorter day, you will have to have more than one solar cooker!)

LET'S GET STARTED!

⌘

CASSEROLES have a large amount of water incorporated into them in order to cook the pastas, grains, and legumes. They can be put into a cold cooker and the whole thing can come to boiling temperature together. Once the contents come to a boil, cooking time will be the same as in a conventional oven, but it may take quite a while to get the whole mass up to boiling temperature. If you are assured of a clear day, and your casserole doesn't require more than 30 minutes of boiling time, you can place it in the solar cooker, turn it to where the sun will be at 2:00, and go away. Dinner will be ready and warm at 5:30 (don't do this with meat or other potentially dangerous food). For longer cooking times, you must turn the solar cooker every 30 minutes or so to keep the contents boiling. Any recipe designed for a slow cooker will do very well in a solar cooker. Note that in general, green things like broccoli and peas will be turned brown by the sun, so either cover them with an opaque lid (which makes the cooking less efficient) or add them to the dish after you remove it from the cooker (better nutrition and fresh taste). Food cut in smaller pieces will cook faster and more evenly.

ANYTHING WHICH CAN BE ROASTED in an oven can be put in a loosely covered jar or covered casserole to roast in its own juices. Potatoes, carrots, turnips, garlic, onions, squash and beets will all turn out juicy and tender. They will not be glazed or browned because they will stay moist in the cooker.

BULGUR WITH GREENS AND CHEESE

Stirring the greens in after baking the bulgur gives this dish a fresh flavor. Use tender spring greens from the garden, if available. Fresh herbs like oregano and basil are great as well, but it will take only 1/4 cup of them.

Serves 2-3:

    1 1/2 cups bulgur
    3 1/4 cups water
    3 cloves garlic, minced
    1/2 teaspoon minced gingerroot
    1 medium carrot, grated coarsely
    1 1/2 tablespoons tamari
    2 cups loosely packed tender greens, shredded, or 1/4 cup chopped
        fresh herbs
    3 ounces jack cheese, diced 1/4-inch

   In a 2-liter or larger casserole, combine the bulgur, water, garlic, gingerroot, tamari, and grated carrot. Bake, covered, in solar cooker until the water is absorbed. Remove from the cooker, stir in the shredded greens or herbs, and replace the cover until the greens are wilted (do not put back in the sun). Stir in the diced cheese immediately before serving.

☼

Conventional kitchen instructions: In a medium saucepan, mix all the ingredients except the greens. Simmer gently, covered, until the water is absorbed and the bulgur is tender, about 20 to 25 minutes. Add the greens, turn off the heat, and let the bulgur sit on the burner for 2 more minutes. Serve hot.

SUMMER BULGUR

Make this dish when the garden is in plenty. Use any kind of summer squash (crookneck, zucchini, pattypan), as long as it is yellow! The sun will turn green squash an unappetizing brown color, unless you have it in an opaque cooking pot.

Serves 3-4:

   13/4 cups bulgur wheat
   31/4 cups stock or water
   3/4 cup chopped tomatoes (fresh or canned)
   2 cups diced yellow summer squash
   1 cup finely-cut cauliflower
   3 or 4 cloves garlic, minced
   2 tablespoons tamari
   1/4 cup chopped fresh basil (or 2 teaspoons dry)

Combine all ingredients in a 2-liter or larger casserole. Bake, covered, in solar cooker until all liquid is absorbed. Stir before serving. Serve hot, or chill and dress with a little oil and vinegar as a salad.

Conventional kitchen instructions: Add 1/4 cup extra liquid for a total of 31/2 cups. Combine all ingredients except the basil in a large saucepan. Bring to a boil over a hot burner, then reduce heat to low, and simmer gently until all liquid is absorbed (about 25 minutes). Add the basil, cover the pan, and let rest 5 minutes. Stir to fluff the bulgur before serving.

BURRITOS WITH RICE AND LENTIL CHILI

Don't feel limited by what's in the recipe: use any vegetables you have. This is supposed to be a simple dish that's adaptable to what you have on hand!

Makes 6 fat burritos:

2/3 cup brown rice
1/4 cup lentils
2 1/2 cups stock or water
3 cloves garlic, minced
1/2 teaspoon minced gingerroot
1 tablespoon chili powder
1/2 teaspoon cumin
1 tablespoon tamari
1/8 teaspoon Tabasco (optional)
1/2 teaspoon oregano
1 large carrot, grated coarsely
1 cup chopped cauliflower
6 whole wheat tortillas

Combine all ingredients except the tortillas in a 2-liter or larger casserole. Cook in solar cooker until all the water is absorbed. Rice and lentils should be tender (if not, adjust the amount of water in the recipe).

Stir well, then serve the filling wrapped in tortillas, garnished with your choice of the following: grated cheese, sliced avocado, guacamole, lettuce, tomatoes, salsa, olives, really hot sauce, fresh cilantro -- you name it. Let your imagination be your guide!

✿

Conventional kitchen instructions: Combine all ingredients except the tortillas in a medium saucepan. Bring to a boil, reduce heat, and simmer gently without stirring until the rice and lentils are tender. To check for doneness, poke a spoon to the bottom of the pot. Move the contents aside. When the liquid is gone from the bottom of the pot, the contents should be tender. If not, pour a little water straight down the hole, replace the lid, and cook a little longer. Use a little more water next time and adjust the recipe.

When the filling is done, stir well. Serve as above.

HERBED POTATOES

A quick and easy main or side dish to make from your root cellar vegetables and home-dried herbs.

Serves 6 as a side dish:

    3 pounds red or yellow potatoes, scrubbed and diced
    1 tablespoon olive oil
    2 cups diced onion
    4 cloves garlic, minced
    1/4 teaspoon celery seed
    1/4 teaspoon dried marjoram
    1/2 teaspoon dried savory
    1/2 teaspoon oregano
    1 small fresh hot pepper, seeds removed, finely diced
    2 tablespoons tamari
    1/2 cup grated kohlrabi or carrot
    1/4 cup vegetable stock

Put all the ingredients in a 2-liter or larger covered casserole. Place in solar cooker and steam until potatoes are tender. Remove from cooker, stir to coat potatoes with sauce, and serve in a bowl or soup plate.

❖

Conventional kitchen instructions: Dice and steam the potatoes till tender. In a large, heavy skillet, cook the onions and garlic in the olive oil until they are tender and transparent. Add all the herbs, the kohlrabi or carrot, and the stock, and simmer gently until the liquid evaporates. Add the cooked potatoes, toss, and serve immediately or keep warm in a 200-degree oven for up to 30 minutes.

CURRIED RICE AND LENTILS

A quick and easy main dish, best served with a big salad on the side. Use either raw or toasted cashews as you prefer.

Serves 4:

1 1/2 cups uncooked brown rice
1/3 cup lentils
4 1/2 cups water
1 1/2 cups diced onion
3 cloves garlic, minced
2 teaspoons fresh gingerroot, minced
1 teaspoon turmeric
1 teaspoon cumin
1/2 teaspoon coriander
1/8 teaspoon cayenne
2-3 tablespoons tamari (to taste)
1/4 cup cashews
2 cups fresh or frozen peas

Combine all ingredients except the cashews and peas in a 2-liter or larger casserole. Bake, covered, in solar cooker until all liquid is absorbed. Rice and lentils should be tender (if not, adjust the liquid amount next time. Additional liquid will make the rice and lentils more tender). Remove from cooker and stir in the cashews and peas. Let sit, covered, for 2 or 3 minutes before serving.

Serve with salad and chutney. Optionally, the cashews may be used as a garnish instead of stirring them in.

Conventional kitchen instructions: Put the rice, lentils and water in a large saucepan and bring to a boil. Reduce the heat and simmer, covered, until the water is absorbed, about 45 minutes.

Meanwhile, heat the olive oil in a medium frying pan and sauté the onions, garlic and gingerroot gently until the onions are transparent. Add the turmeric, cumin, coriander and cayenne and "toast" the spices for a few moments. Scrape the mixture into the cooked rice and lentils, add the cashews and peas, stir well, then let sit for 2 or 3 minutes before serving as above.

BLACKEYED PEAS AND RICE

Blackeyed peas and rice are a traditional Southern combination. Combine them with plenty of vegetables and season "just right" for an easy-to-fix meal. The greens are a traditional touch. Use whatever kind of tender greens you have in your garden or the store: turnip, beet, chard, mustard, etc.

Serves 3:
    1 cup diced onion
    1 tablespoon olive oil
    11/2 cups uncooked brown rice
    1/3 cup black-eyed peas, picked over and washed
    5 cups water
    2 tablespoons tamari
    1/4 teaspoon Tabasco
    1/2 teaspoon ground coriander
    2 carrots, sliced or diced 1/2-inch
    1 white turnip, sliced or diced 1/2-inch
    1 bay leaf
    1/2 teaspoon dry thyme
    1 bunch greens (see above), washed and shredded 1-inch

Combine all ingredients except the greens in a 2-liter or larger covered casserole. Place in solar cooker, and cook until all the water is absorbed. Remove the casserole from the cooker, stir in the greens, and replace the cover on the dish. Let sit for 5 minutes (do not put back in the sun). Stir and serve.

Conventional kitchen instructions: In a large saucepan or Dutch oven over medium heat, sauté the onions in the olive oil until transparent, adding a little water as necessary to keep from sticking. Wash the black-eyed peas and add to onions, and then add the rice and 5 cups of water. Add the tamari, Tabasco, coriander, carrots and turnip. Stir together.

Bring the pot to a boil, lower the heat, and simmer, covered, for 45 minutes **without stirring**. Remove the cover and taste the beans and rice. They should be tender. Poke a spoon to the bottom of the pot, and if there is less than 1/4 inch of liquid on the bottom, add 1/4 cup of water. Add the bay leaf, thyme, and greens, then stir. Turn the heat as low as it will go, and cook for 5 more minutes, stirring **frequently**. Once you stir the pot and release the starch from the rice, it will tend to stick. As soon as the greens are wilted and minimally cooked, remove the pot from the stove.

Serve immediately, garnished with grated cheese and salsa if desired.

EIGHT-LAYER DIP

Use this for a chip-dip, or serve it as a main course for two with tortillas.

Serves 2 as a main course:
    2 cups seasoned beans (see below)
    1/4 cup sliced green onions
    1 cup grated jack cheese
    1/2 cup sliced olives
    1 cup salsa
    1/2 cup sour cream
    1/2 cup guacamole or mashed avocado
    1/4 cup fresh cilantro, roughly chopped

Spread the seasoned beans in the bottom of a 11/2-liter or larger covered casserole. Over them, layer the green onions, grated cheese, sliced olives, and salsa. Cover the casserole, and heat in the solar cooker until the cheese is melted and everything begins to bubble. Remove from cooker and add layers of sour cream, guacamole and cilantro. Serve immediately with corn chips or tortillas.

Conventional kitchen instructions: Prepare as above. Bake in a preheated 350-degree oven until bubbling, about 15 to 20 minutes.

✿

SEASONED BEANS

Quick beans for burritos, dips, and recipes calling for refried beans. See **Basic Beans** (p. 25), for tips on cooked beans.

Makes 2 cups:
    2 cups cooked and mashed pinto, black or red beans (about 1 cup dry)
    1 clove garlic, pressed
    1/2 teaspoon chili powder
    1 tablespoon tamari, or to taste
    Bean cooking liquid if needed

Stir together the beans, garlic, chili and tamari. Add enough of the bean cooking liquid to make a creamy consistency if you desire. If the beans are cold and stiff, they will get softer when heated.

SPANISH RICE

This rice is better than that bland, orange-colored stuff you get in Mexican restaurants. Its flavor is sweetened and intensified by cooking in the sun! Long grain rice comes out fluffier than short grain.

Serves 4-6:

    1 teaspoon olive oil
    3/4 cup chopped onions
    2 cloves garlic, minced
    13/4 cups uncooked brown rice
    31/4 cups water
    1 cup chopped tomatoes (fresh or canned)
    1/2 teaspoon chili powder
    1 tablespoon tamari
    1/4 teaspoon cumin

Combine all ingredients in a 2-liter or larger covered casserole. Place in solar cooker, and bake until water is absorbed and rice is tender. Let rest 5 minutes in casserole after removing from cooker. Fluff up rice, and serve.

⊕

Conventional kitchen instructions: Increase the olive oil to 1 tablespoon. Cook the onions and garlic in the oil over medium heat until transparent, adding a little water as necessary to keep from sticking. Add the other ingredients and cook, without stirring, until the water is absorbed and the rice is tender (about 50 minutes). Serve as above.

MAMA GIANNA'S EASY VEGIE LASAGNA

This is a one-dish lasagna with nothing precooked. Make this lasagna in a 2-liter or larger covered casserole. You must use a covered casserole because the noodles need the steam to cook! This is great with whole wheat lasagna noodles. Note that most of the cheese is not on the top! Cheese directly exposed to the sun will turn to leather. Put it in the middle of your casseroles, and add more to the top only near the end.

Serves 3-4:

Sauce: 1 28-ounce can ground, chopped or crushed tomatoes
1/2 cup water
1 tablespoon red wine
3 cloves garlic, minced
1 teaspoon oregano
1/2 teaspoon basil
1/4 teaspoon fennel seed, crushed
1 tablespoon tamari
Veggies:1 medium carrot, grated
1 green pepper, diced
1/2 cup diced onion
Cheese:1 cup Ricotta
1/4 cup Parmesan
1 egg, beaten
Fresh-ground black pepper to taste
Grated Mozzarella for topping (optional)
Noodles:8-10 lasagna noodles, or enough to make two complete layers

Set your solar cooker out to preheat, and get out a 2-liter or larger covered casserole. In a medium bowl, mix together the sauce ingredients. In another medium bowl, toss together the prepared vegetables. In a small bowl, stir together the cheeses, egg and pepper.
Layer ingredients as follows:
1/3 of the sauce
Layer of uncooked noodles
All the vegetables
1/3 of the sauce
All of the cheese mixture
Layer of uncooked noodles
1/3 of the sauce
Cover the casserole with a lid. Bake in solar cooker until the casserole has bubbled vigorously for 30 minutes (it takes two hours or more to bring it to the boil, but once things are boiling the cooking time is the same in a solar cooker as in a conventional oven). When the noodles are cooked, remove the lid and

add a layer of grated mozzarella. Bake 15 to 20 minutes more, uncovered, until the cheese bubbles and browns. Let rest 10 minutes before serving.

Conventional kitchen instructions: Bake 11/2 hours, covered, in a preheated 350-degree oven. Remove the lid, add the cheese, and continue as above.

❖

RISOTTO

This is a baked Italian-style rice dish. If you cannot get fresh oregano and lovage, follow the substitutions for "winter risotto."

Serves 4:

    12/3 cups uncooked brown rice
    2 tablespoons lentils
    11/2 cups chopped, ground, or crushed tomatoes
    22/3 cups stock or water
    1 small onion, sliced thin
    2 cloves garlic, minced
    1 small turnip, coarsely grated
    1/3 cup chopped fresh oregano
    2 teaspoons finely chopped fresh lovage leaf
    Dash Tabasco
    1/4 teaspoon ground cumin
    1 tablespoon olive oil
    1 tablespoon tamari

Winter Risotto: delete fresh oregano and lovage, and substitute:
    2 teaspoons dried oregano, crushed
    1/2 teaspoon fennel seed, crushed or ground

Combine ingredients in a 2-liter or larger casserole. Stir to mix. Bake, covered, in solar cooker until all liquid is absorbed. The rice and lentils should be tender (if not, adjust liquid amount next time). When it is done, the herbs will be on the top. Stir everything together before serving.
Serve with a crusty bread and green salad.

Conventional kitchen instructions: Preheat oven to 350 degrees. Combine all ingredients in a 2-liter or larger casserole. Stir to mix. Bake, covered, until the liquid is absorbed and the rice and lentils are tender, about 2 hours.

BARBECUE BEANS

Tender little beans in a sweet-and-sour barbecue sauce. Great as a main dish with cornbread and green salad, or as a side dish with your favorite barbecue.

Serves 4-6:

> 2 cups small white beans
> 2 cups chili sauce, preferably homemade
> 1 tablespoon tamari
> 1/4 teaspoon Tabasco sauce (or more if you like it hot)
> 3 tablespoons honey
> 1/4 cup lemon juice
> 1/2 cup bean cooking liquid
> 2 tablespoons tomato paste
> 1 tablespoon cider vinegar
> 1 tablespoon arrowroot

Pick over and wash the beans. Soak them overnight in plenty of water. Discard the soaking water, rinse the beans, and put in a 2-liter or larger casserole with plenty of water to cover. Simmer the beans gently in solar cooker until tender.

When the beans are tender, drain and save the cooking water. Add the rest of the ingredients to the casserole, using some of the cooking water in the recipe. Stir well to dissolve arrowroot completely. Return to solar cooker, and simmer until the sauce thickens, at least 20 minutes after you see it bubble. More cooking will not hurt this, especially if you let the sun pass it by after a while and it stays just barely simmering.

⊕

Conventional kitchen instructions: Follow solar cooker instructions except, simmer the beans on the stovetop in a large saucepan until tender. Do not add arrowroot to the rest of the ingredients at first. Bring all except arrowroot to a boil, reduce heat, and simmer 20 minutes to blend the flavors.

Mix the arrowroot with a little water in a cup. Remove a spoonful or two of the sauce, and stir into the arrowroot mixture. Scrape the mixture into the simmering pot, stirring constantly to distribute evenly as it thickens. When thick, you may keep hot on the lowest stove setting until ready to serve. The beans will continue getting better!

TAMALE PIE

A rousing red bean chili topped with tender Jalapeño cornbread. It is necessary to have precooked beans for this recipe. This recipe illustrates the technique of cooking a sauce or stew, then topping with cake or quickbread.

Serves 3-4:
   1 cup diced onions
   1 1/2 cups cooked red beans (see **Basic Beans**, p. 25)
   1 28-ounce can chopped tomatoes (1 3/4 cups)
   4 cloves garlic, minced
   1 tablespoon chili powder
   1 teaspoon ground cumin
   1 tablespoon dried oregano, crushed
   Dash cayenne powder
   1 tablespoon tamari
Cornbread topping:
   2 eggs
   1/3 cup olive oil
   1 cup yogurt
   1 cup corn kernels (frozen or fresh)
   1 cup cornmeal
   3 teaspoons baking powder
   1/4 teaspoon salt
   2 tablespoons finely-chopped Jalapeño pepper
   1/2 cup grated Jack cheese

   To make the filling: Combine all ingredients in a 2-liter or larger covered casserole. Place in solar cooker, bring to the boil and simmer 1 hour or until flavors are well-blended. Meanwhile, make the cornbread topping.
   Cornbread topping: In a large bowl, beat the eggs, olive oil, and yogurt together. Add the corn kernels. In a separate bowl, stir together the cornmeal, baking powder and salt. Stir into the wet mixture only enough to moisten all ingredients. Stir in the chopped peppers and cheese.
   Remove the casserole from the solar cooker and set the lid aside. Scrape the cornbread topping over the bubbling chili. Put back in the solar cooker, uncovered, and bake until the bread is done (it will turn golden on top, and be firm to the touch). Serve hot, by spooning chili over the cornbread.

Conventional kitchen instructions: Simmer the bean mixture in a medium saucepan, covered, over low heat for about 45 minutes or until the onions are tender, the sauce is thick, and flavors are well-blended. Stir frequently to prevent sticking. Pour the sauce into a 2-liter or larger casserole, top with the cornbread batter, and bake 25 to 30 minutes in a preheated 350-degree oven, until the topping is golden and tests done.

SHEPHERD'S PIE

A traditional English main-dish pie topped with potatoes.

Serves 2-3:

  1 cup diced onions
  3/4 cup brown lentils
  2 cups water or stock
  2 tablespoons tamari
  1 cup shredded cabbage
  1 medium carrot, diced (1/2 cup)
  1/2 cup diced turnip or 1 cup chopped cauliflower
  1/2 teaspoon dried savory
  3-4 cups leftover mashed potatoes
  Paprika
  Black pepper

Place the onions, lentils, water or stock, tamari, cabbage, carrot, turnip or cauliflower, and savory in a 2-liter or larger covered casserole. Give it all a stir, put the lid on, then bake in solar cooker until the lentils are tender and the water absorbed (about 1 hour after it begins to simmer). Take the casserole out, stir the mixture, and spoon the leftover potatoes over the top. Sprinkle the potatoes with a little paprika and/or black pepper to season, cover the casserole again, and return to the solar cooker. Bake until the potatoes are piping hot and puffed up, with the sauce bubbling up around the edges. Serve hot.

Conventional kitchen instructions: In a medium saucepan on the stovetop, sauté onions in 1 tablespoon olive oil until transparent. Add lentils, stock, tamari, cabbage, carrot, turnip or cauliflower, and savory. Simmer until the lentils are tender, about 45 minutes. Scrape the mixture into a 2-liter or larger casserole and top with the potatoes as above. Bake in a preheated 350-degree oven, covered, about 20 minutes more.

Hint: If your lentils persist in coming out chewy, soak them overnight in water. Drain and cook as above, reducing the amount of stock or water by half. If you don't have leftover potatoes, you may use reconstituted instant potatoes.

PESTO ROLY-POLY

This one is like a rolled up pesto pizza.

Makes a 5X9-inch loaf, or lunch for 4:

Dough:
> 1 1/2 cups warm water
> 1 tablespoon dry yeast
> 1/2 teaspoon honey
> 1 tablespoon olive oil
> 1/2 teaspoon salt
> 3-4 cups whole wheat bread flour

Pesto:
> 1/3 cup olive oil
> 4 cloves garlic
> 1 tablespoon tamari
> 2 cups packed basil leaves
> also:
> 4 large brown mushrooms, diced (optional)
> 1/2 cup cubed Jack, Cheddar or Mozzarella cheese

In a large bowl, dissolve the yeast with the honey in the warm water. Set aside for 10 minutes. When the yeast foams, add the oil, salt and enough bread flour to make a stiff dough. Cover and let rise for 30 minutes while you make the pesto.

For the pesto, combine the olive oil, garlic, tamari and basil in a blender or food processor. Process, turning the machine off and pushing the leaves down onto the blades as necessary, until smooth.

Set your solar cooker out to preheat. Lightly oil a 5X9-inch loaf pan. Set aside. Turn the dough out onto a floured board and knead until smooth and springy, about 5 to 7 minutes. Roll out to an oblong about 9X15 inches. Spread the dough with the pesto, and sprinkle the mushrooms and cheese over it. Starting with a short edge, roll the dough up into a 9-inch long loaf. Place the loaf in the pan. Let rise until increased in bulk by 50 percent.

Bake in solar cooker until the loaf tests done. Serve hot or cool.

❖

Conventional kitchen instructions: Bake in a preheated 350-degree oven for 40 to 50 minutes, until the loaf tests done.

LIMA BEAN AND SAGE CHOWDER

A savory soup for fall and winter.

Serves 4:

    2 1/3 cups cooked small white lima beans (about 1 cup dry)
    1 cup diced onion
    1 medium carrot, halved and sliced
    1 pound boiling potatoes, diced
    1/8 teaspoon celery seed
    1 bay leaf
    1 teaspoon rubbed sage
    1 tablespoon tamari
    2-3 cups stock or water
    2 tablespoons water
    2 tablespoons fine whole wheat flour

Cook the beans as in **Basic Beans** (p.25), or use canned. Put the beans into a 2-liter or larger covered casserole. Add the onion, carrot, and potatoes to the casserole, but keep the level 1/2 inch below the rim. Add the celery seed, bay leaf, sage, and tamari. Add the stock or water to just cover the vegetables, stirring all together. Cover, place in solar cooker, and simmer until the vegetables are tender.

In a small cup, combine the water and flour to make a smooth paste. Remove some of the soup stock from the pot and mix with the paste, then return the mixture to the casserole, stirring well to blend.

Return to the cooker and simmer until the soup thickens. Serve immediately with a fresh salad or green garnish, and plenty of homemade bread!

Conventional kitchen instructions: In a large stockpot, sauté the onion in 1 tablespoon olive oil, covered, until beginning to brown around the edges. Add the prepared carrot, potatoes, celery seed, bay leaf, sage, and tamari. Add the stock or water, bring to a boil, adjust heat to simmer, and cook until the vegetables are just tender (about 30 minutes). Mix the flour paste as above, and simmer about 5 minutes more until thick.

RED SOUP

Serve with a dollop of yogurt and a sprinkle of dill weed for a traditional touch. Good with rye bread, too.

Makes 4 servings:

    1 cup diced onion (about 1 medium)
    1 cup shredded golden turnip (1 medium-small)
    1 cup shredded carrot (2 medium)
    1 1/2 cups shredded beet (1 medium-large)
    1 cup shredded red cabbage
    1 15-ounce can crushed tomatoes or 1 3/4 cups chopped fresh tomatoes
    2 cups stock or water
    2 tablespoons tomato paste
    1-2 teaspoons honey
    1 tablespoon tamari
    2 tablespoons lemon juice

Combine all ingredients except the lemon juice in a 2-liter or larger casserole. Stir to combine, and smooth the vegetables down into the liquid. Cook in solar cooker until the soup has bubbled for at least 1 hour. Remove from cooker and stir well. Stir in lemon juice, and taste to see if seasoning needs to be adjusted. Serve hot.

⊕

Conventional kitchen instructions: Heat 1 tablespoon olive oil in a medium stockpot or Dutch oven. Add onion and sauté until soft. Add turnip, carrots, beets, cabbage and a little water; and sauté another 10 minutes. Add more water if the vegetables start to stick.

Add tomatoes, stock or water, tomato paste, honey and tamari. Bring to a boil, lower heat to simmer, and cook, covered, until vegetables are tender, about 30 minutes. Stir in lemon juice, and taste to see if seasoning needs to be adjusted. Serve hot.

CURRIED RED LENTIL SOUP

This soup is made of root vegetables and standard kitchen ingredients, so its a great one to keep the makings on-hand for. It has a lovely golden color.

Serves 2-3:

 1 cup red lentils
 22/3 cups water
 3 medium potatoes, peeled and diced 1/2-inch
 1 medium carrot, diced
 1 cup diced onion
 3 cloves garlic, minced
 1 teaspoon turmeric
 11/2 teaspoons ground cumin
 1 teaspoon ground coriander
 1/8 teaspoon cayenne pepper
 1 tablespoon tamari

Pick over the lentils and put in a strainer. Rinse under cold running water. Combine all ingredients in a 2-liter or larger casserole. Stir well and cover. Put in solar cooker, and cook until lentils are tender and disintegrating. Stir well before serving.

This is delicious served with a dollop of yogurt on top.

Conventional kitchen instructions: Cook the lentils in a medium saucepan with the 22/3 cups water. Bring to a boil and simmer, uncovered, for 20 minutes over low heat. Stir occasionally. Lentils should be tender.

Add the diced potatoes and carrots, and stir to blend. Continue cooking. Meanwhile, heat 1 tablespoon olive oil in a small skillet. Add the onion, garlic, and all of the spices. Add a small amount of water as necessary to keep from sticking. Cook for 3 minutes, or until the onions begin to get tender.

Add the onion to the soup, stir, and cook until the potatoes are tender, about 20 more minutes. Add the tamari. If the soup is too thick, thin with a little water.

Note: Although this soup tastes great at this stage, it is even better reheated!

TEMPEH STEW

This is a wonderful vegetarian stew with a savory miso gravy.

Serves 2-3:

    1 clove garlic, minced
    1 medium onion
    1 8-ounce cake of tempeh
    2 cups water
    2 carrots, diced
    2 large potatoes, diced
    1-2 turnips, diced
    1 teaspoon prepared mustard
    2 tablespoons miso
    1/4 teaspoon rosemary
    1/2 teaspoon thyme
    1/2 teaspoon marjoram
    1/2 teaspoon sage
    1 tablespoon arrowroot or 2 tablespoons flour

In a 2-liter or larger covered glass casserole, combine the tempeh, water, diced vegetables, and garlic. Stir them together and cook in a solar cooker until the vegetables are tender (this means about 30 minutes of simmering, after everything comes to the boil).

Stir in the mustard, miso and herbs. Dissolve the arrowroot or flour in 1/4 cup of water and add it to the casserole, stirring well. Close the solar cooker and bring back to the boil. Simmer about 15 minutes more, until thick, then stir and serve.

☯

Conventional kitchen instructions: In a 3-liter or larger stockpot or Dutch oven, warm 2 tablespoons olive oil over medium heat and sauté the onion until it is translucent. Add the tempeh and garlic, then stir-fry briefly.

Now add the water and the diced carrots, potatoes and turnip. Stir them together and simmer until the vegetables are tender, about 20 minutes after everything comes to the boil (if you dice the vegetables smaller, they will cook more quickly).

Stir in the mustard, miso and herbs. Simmer for about 10 minutes more. Dissolve the arrowroot or flour in 1/4 cup of water and add it to the pot, stirring well. Simmer about 5 minutes more, stirring frequently.

MEXICAN POTATO STEW

The greens in this stew are added after baking, and wilted in the heat of the sauce. If you like to collect wild greens, you may use them in place of the spinach. This is delicious with cornbread.

Serves 3-4:

    1 medium onion, diced
    1 jalapeno pepper, seeds removed, finely diced
    13/4 cup chopped fresh tomatoes
      (or 1 15-ounce can)
    11/2 pounds potatoes, scrubbed and diced
    3 medium carrots, scrubbed and diced
    1 tablespoon tamari
    1 cup loosely-packed tender chard or spinach, chopped
      (stems chopped very fine)

Place all the ingredients except the greens in a 2-liter or larger covered casserole. Bake in solar cooker until the potatoes are so tender they are splitting. Remove the casserole from the cooker and fold the greens into the sauce. Replace the lid on the casserole and let rest for 5 minutes. Do not put the casserole back into the cooker. Serve hot.

Conventional kitchen instructions: In a medium saucepan, heat 1 tablespoon olive oil and add the onion and pepper. Sauté gently over medium heat until the onion is golden. Add the tomatoes, potatoes, carrots and tamari. Cover and cook over medium-low heat until potatoes are tender, about 15 minutes. Check the amount of liquid, and add more if necessary. There should be about 1/4 cup.

Add the greens, cover, and cook over medium heat until they are tender, about 3 minutes. Toss the vegetables to distribute the sauce. Serve immediately.

BASIC BEANS

When a recipe calls for cooked beans, canned beans may be used. You may, however, prefer to make cooked beans from dried beans because of ease of storing the dried ones, or because of the low cost of dried beans when compared to canned ones. Cooking beans with the sun is easy, as long as you have a little spare time. They don't boil over in a solar cooker, and they come out sweet and tender.

Only lentils and black-eyed peas can be cooked with no pre-soaking. To soak any of the others, first pick them over for stones and defective beans, then rinse them and cover them with plenty of lukewarm water. Beans are living seeds, with the two halves of the bean being the cotyledons, or first leaves, which provide the nutrients for the initial phase of plant growth. Soaking them in 80- to 90-degree water makes them begin to sprout and grow, which starts the process of turning the starches into sugars needed for growth. This makes for a sweeter, easier-to-digest bean.

Let the beans soak overnight. If you can't possibly do this, then use the quick soak method: bring the beans and plenty of water to a boil, simmer 1 minute, then remove from heat and let soak for 1 hour.

When the beans are soaked, rinse and drain them well, discarding the soaking water. Put them in your cooking pot, casserole, or jar. Cover with plenty of fresh water. Beans will expand 2 to 2 1/2 times their original volume. The lid of your cooking container should be vented or attached loosely to allow steam to escape.

Use this chart to determine how much cooking time each type of bean will take. The variation in cooking times shows that some types of bean are more practical than others for solar cookery. Very dry or old beans will take longer to cook than freshly dried ones. Check to see that the top of the beans remains covered by water during the entire cooking time.

Variety	Cooking Time
Lentils, red (pink)	40 minutes
Lentils, brown	45 minutes
Black-eyed peas	1 hour
Small red beans	1 hour
Lima Beans	1 hour
Pinto beans	2 hours
Red kidney beans	2 hours
Black beans	2 hours
Garbanzo beans	3 hours

EASY BROWN RICE

My husband likes to make this so that when I come home from work in the summer, all I have to do for dinner is forage for stir-fry ingredients in the garden. A few minutes over the regular stove, and dinner is ready!

Serves 4:

 2 cups uncooked brown rice
 4 cups water

Combine the rice and water in a 2-liter or larger covered casserole. Cook in solar cooker until done (water is all absorbed), then serve immediately, close lid to keep warm until needed, or chill for a cold salad (see **Curried Rice Salad**, p.29).

Conventional kitchen instructions: Place the rice and the water in a covered saucepan, and bring to a boil. Lower the heat until the water is simmering rapidly, and cook, covered, for about 45 minutes or until all the water is absorbed. Now here's the secret: DO NOT STIR. Remove the lid as many times as you want, to check the rice. Listen for the sound of the bubbling water. Take a spoon and just poke it straight down through the rice, and push a little bit to the side to look at the bottom of the pan and see if the water is absorbed. But do not stir the rice.

The reason for this is: the steam, as it cooks, makes little tunnels up through the rice. If you stir the rice, you release the starch in it. It combines with the water to make a gummy paste, which keeps the steam from transferring heat up through the mixture to the top. Result: the bottom burns, the top doesn't cook, and the liquid which should be available to cook the rice is bound up with the starch in a gummy mass.

When the liquid is all absorbed into the rice, taste a few grains. If they are not quite done, add a small amount of liquid and replace the cover on the pot. Cook for another 5 minutes, and repeat the tests for doneness

Solar Salads

MUDDY ROADS AND SPRING GARDENING

Our back road has turned to a ribbon of slush and mud. Our pine woods are still full of snowbanks over two-feet deep. During the past five years, the average appearance of the first buttercup blossom is March 20th. It's the Ides of March today (the 15th), and nary a buttercup leaf shows its green tip in the few spots of bare earth.

Lance stands in the garden and surveys his work. "I'm sure glad we don't live in one of those short-season areas where we can't even get started on our gardening until later on," he says. We had a spell of hot weather last week, and the intense March sun began to thaw the soil underneath the snow. When the edges of the snowbanks started to pull back from the warming earth, Lance's green thumbs began to twitch. He already had cabbages and lettuces started in the house in anticipation.

We worked on the 24-foot-long bed where we hope to plant the onion starts that will arrive in a few short weeks. Lance had already shoveled it out, and the soil was thawed. We hooped it up and stretched a row cover over the hoops to moderate the temperature inside and help the soil continue warming. We planted lettuce on the Ides of March last year, and by May 1st, we were eating all the green salads we wanted.

In our climate, it's not a matter of waiting a week or two until the soil is warm and the weather more clement. Spring comes only reluctantly, and fully one third of the sunny half of the year will pass before we can plant even frost-tolerant species without protection. Tender varieties will wait many years for a suitable summer in this, the coldest place in Washington and Oregon. Starting early and persisting long into the fall is the only way we can grow our garden full of food.

Of course, some people around here think we are crazy trying to stretch the limits of the seasons. And it's true, some plants don't make it and some experiments fail. Our worst freeze actually happened in the middle of June a few summers ago. It was the worst because the plants had become accustomed to warm summer-like weather, and were not frost-hardened as they become in spring and fall. Some of the plants in the garden were killed outright, and some set back so they never recovered.

But from that experience we learned valuable lessons. We learned that a little insignificant broccoli-like oriental green (named Tsai Shim) could take frost like no other vegetable, and we learned that China Choy planted after the summer solstice (as an emergency crop to quickly replace frozen ones) had much less tendency to bolt than the same crop planted in spring.

So now when Lance says, "What do you think of this idea? Shall I try it?" I say, "Sure, go ahead!" and I think how little we have to lose, and how much we have to gain. A few plants or a day's work is a small price to pay when our most important harvest is knowledge.

...from "Morning Hill News" #40, March/April '98

28

CURRIED RICE SALAD

Cook the rice any time and stick it in the fridge. Then make this salad ahead for a carefree meal.

Serves 4 as a main dish:

> 13/4 cups uncooked brown rice
> 31/2 cups water
> 1/3 cup finely diced dried apricots
> 1/2 cup raw cashews, toasted*
> 2 cups bok choi, sliced

Dressing:
> 1/2 cup mayonnaise
> 2/3 cup yogurt
> 21/2 teaspoons curry powder
> 2 cloves garlic, minced
> 1 teaspoon minced fresh gingerroot
> Pinch cayenne pepper

Cook the rice, following instructions for **Easy Brown Rice** (p.26). Cool the rice in the refrigerator until well-chilled before proceeding with the rest of the recipe.

Put the apricots, cashews and greens in a large bowl with the rice. Mix the dressing ingredients in a small bowl, and pour over the rice in the large bowl. Toss all well to combine. Chill at least 2 hours before serving. This keeps well for 2 or 3 days.

For an elegant presentation, save out the prettiest bok choi leaves, and use a higher proportion of stems in the salad. Dress the leaves lightly with oil and vinegar, and arrange them on a shallow dish or platter with the rice salad on top of them.

☯

*To toast cashews: Spread the cashews on a pie plate or cookie sheet. Toast in a preheated solar cooker or 350-degree oven for 5 to 10 minutes, until lightly golden.

"RAD" RICE SALAD

A rice salad with crunchy root vegetables and a savory dressing. Use long-grain rice for a fluffy salad, and unsulphured apricots for their intense flavor.

Serves 4 as a main dish:

    13/4 cups brown rice
    31/2 cups water
    1 stalk celery, with leaves, thinly sliced
    1/3 cup finely slivered dried apricots
    1/4 cup sliced hazelnuts
    1 cup red radishes, thinly sliced
    1 cup shredded Savoy cabbage
    1 small orange, peeled, sectioned, and cut into 1/4-inch pieces
    1/3 cup cilantro, roughly chopped

Dressing:
    1/3 cup olive oil
    2 tablespoons balsamic vinegar
    2 tablespoons brown rice vinegar
    1 tablespoon tamari
    1 tablespoon honey
    1/4 teaspoon grated orange peel (fresh or dried)

Cook the rice, following instructions for **Easy Brown Rice** (p.26). Cool the rice in the refrigerator until well-chilled before proceeding with the rest of the recipe.

Prepare the fruits and vegetables, and put them with the rice in a large bowl. Mix the dressing ingredients and pour over the rice, fruits and vegetables. Toss well to combine all ingredients. Chill at least 2 hours before serving to allow the flavors to mingle.

RANCH POTATO SALAD

A hearty Western-style potato salad.

Serves 6 as a side dish:
  2 lbs. waxy potatoes, diced
  1/3 cup diced cucumber
  1/3 cup diced celery
  1/4 cup coarsely grated carrot
  1/4 cup sliced black olives
  A few olives for garnish
  3/4 cup **Creamy Herb Dressing**, below

Scrub the potatoes, peel if desired (I leave the peel on for more flavor), and dice. Put them in a covered casserole with a few tablespoons of stock or water. Steam in the solar cooker until tender (about 20 minutes boiling time). Drain. Chill the potatoes thoroughly before combining with other ingredients.

Prepare the **Creamy Herb Dressing** with 2 cloves of garlic. Combine the potatoes, cucumber, celery, carrot, olives and 3/4 cup dressing in a bowl. Toss to coat ingredients with dressing. Taste, and adjust amount of dressing or add salt if desired.

Conventional kitchen instructions: Steam the potatoes in a steamer basket over boiling water, or boil them if preferred.

CREAMY HERB DRESSING

A homemade version of the thick buttermilk-and-herb dressing that is far better than store-bought. It makes a great dressing for fresh green salads, too!

Makes 1 cup:
  1/2 cup yogurt
  1/2 cup mayonnaise
  1 teaspoon honey
  1 or 2 cloves garlic (to taste), pressed
  2 teaspoons finely chopped fresh basil
  2 teaspoons finely chopped fresh oregano
  2 teaspoons finely chopped fresh thyme or lemon thyme
  (If you don't have fresh herbs, use approx. 3/4 teaspoon dry herb for each
    kind).

In a small bowl or 2-cup measure, whisk all ingredients together until well-blended. Transfer to a glass jar for storage. Chill at least 1 hour before using.

BLACK-EYED PEAS WITH MUSTARD DRESSING

A simple bean salad. Serve with lots of home-made bread for a quick lunch.

Serves 6 as a side dish:

> 11/2 cups uncooked black-eyed peas
> 3 green onions, sliced thinly
> 2 cups sliced celery
> Sliced olives for garnish (optional)

Dressing:
> 1/3 cup olive oil
> 1 teaspoon lemon juice
> 1 clove garlic, minced
> 2 tablespoons cider vinegar
> 1 teaspoon Dijon mustard
> 1 teaspoon tamari
> Freshly ground black pepper

Pick over and rinse the black-eyed peas. Add peas and 1 quart of water to a covered cooking container. Simmer in solar cooker until the peas are tender. Meanwhile, whisk together the dressing ingredients in a 11/2-quart or larger bowl. Drain the cooked peas well. Put the warm peas to soak in the dressing for 30 minutes, then add the green onions and sliced celery. Chill well. Serve on a bed of lettuce, garnish with sliced olives.

Conventional kitchen instructions: Cook the black-eyed peas in plenty of boiling water until tender, about 20 minutes. Save the bean water for stock. Continue as above.

ORIENTAL BULGUR SALAD

This quick and delicious salad is a standard around our house for taking to potlucks! Use tender young pak chois or mild mustard greens.

Serves 4 as a main dish:

    2 cups bulgur wheat
    2 cups sliced pak choi or greens
    1 clove garlic, minced
    2 green onions, sliced thin
    1/2 cup cilantro leaves
    1 teaspoon gingerroot, minced finely
    1/4 cup dark sesame oil
    1/4 cup tamari
    2 tablespoons balsamic vinegar
    1 1/2 teaspoons honey
    1/4 teaspoon Tabasco
    Toasted cashews as garnish

Boil a quart of water in your solar cooker or on your stovetop.

In a large bowl, cover the bulgur with boiling water and let soak 20 minutes. Taste, and if it has soaked up all the water and is still not tender, add a little more boiling water and let soak until tender. If you add too much water for the bulgur to soak up, you will have to drain it in a sieve. Let cool to room temperature.

Dice the leafy part of the greens into coarse pieces, and slice the tender parts of the stems finely. Place the greens in the bowl with the bulgur. Prepare the garlic, green onions, cilantro leaves and gingerroot, then add them to the bowl.

Sauce: Combine the sesame oil, tamari, balsamic vinegar, honey and Tabasco. Whisk well, and pour it over the bulgur and vegetables. Stir to combine thoroughly. Chill before serving.

☯

Following are some recipes for uncooked salads, which are included because they complement the food in this book well:

❖

THAI CUCUMBER SALAD

This is not a cooked dish at all, rather a fresh, quick, and easy accompaniment to the Oriental main dishes in this book.

Serves 4:

    1 large cucumber, peeled and sliced thin
    1 teaspoon very finely-minced gingerroot
    1 teaspoon dark sesame oil
    1 tablespoon rice vinegar
    Dab of honey (optional)

    Combine all ingredients in a small nonreactive bowl. Cover, and chill in the refrigerator for 2 hours before serving.

❖

JAPANESE "PICKLE" SALAD

Our Sunrise Enterprises Oriental Seeds catalog calls any marinated vegetables "pickles." Grow some bean sprouts in a jar. Add some fresh greens and cilantro, and you have a salad.

Serves 4:

Marinade:
> 1 tablespoon dark sesame oil
> 11/2 teaspoons balsamic vinegar
> 1 teaspoon honey

Vegetables:
> 1 small hot pepper, finely sliced
> 1/2 cup coarsely grated daikon
> 1/2 cup coarsely grated carrot
> 1 cup shredded bok choy or other fresh oriental greens
> 1/2 cup bean sprouts
> 1/4 cup cilantro leaves

Mix the marinade ingredients and add the sliced hot pepper, grated daikon and carrot. Refrigerate at least 2 hours. Just before serving, add the greens, bean sprouts and cilantro leaves. Toss and serve.

QUICK WINTER SALAD

I serve this salad with almost anything when lettuce is expensive. If you don't have a pet potted tomato in your south window, you can skip the tomato.

Serves 2-4:

> 1 carrot, scrubbed and coarsely grated
> 1/2 cup thinly shredded red or Savoy cabbage
> 1/2 cup alfalfa sprouts
> 1 Jerusalem artichoke or 1 kohlrabi, scrubbed and coarsely grated (optional)

Dressing:
> 2 teaspoon lightly toasted sesame oil
> 1 teaspoon rice vinegar
> 1 teaspoon tamari
> 1 **drop** Tabasco

Garnish:
> 1 ripe tomato, chunked, or 2 cherry tomatoes, halved

Toss all the vegetables together except for the tomato. Combine the dressing ingredients and toss with the vegetables (or just use **Creamy Herb Dressing**, p.31). Garnish with tomato, if desired.

❀

CARROT-RAISIN SALAD

This salad is an American basic, and with good reason! The ingredients are very simple and always available. It stores well. And you can always take it with you to potlucks, picnics, parties, or enjoy it at home!

Serves 4:

    21/2 cups coarsely grated raw carrots
    1/2 cup raisins
    2 teaspoons fresh lemon juice
    1/3 cup plain lowfat yogurt
    1-2 teaspoons maple syrup (to taste)

Toss the carrots lightly with the raisins and lemon juice. Blend the yogurt and honey, and stir into the carrot mixture. Chill at least 30 minutes before serving.

⊕

Russian Variation: Omit maple syrup and raisins. Add 1 tablespoon finely chopped onion, 1/4 cup frozen peas, and 1/4 teaspoon dill weed.

CABBAGE-CARROT SLAW
with Honey-mustard Dressing

This quick salad is a great one to make in a hurry, and the ingredients can be kept around for weeks in the refrigerator. You can use either plain green or white round cabbages or for a change use a curly savoy head. Small, tender heads or inner leaves make the best salad.

Serves 6-8:

    4 cups finely shredded cabbage
    11/2 cups coarsely grated carrot (about 2 medium)

    Toss the shredded vegetables together. Make the dressing below (or any other you prefer). Toss, chill, and serve.

HONEY-MUSTARD DRESSING

This makes a good dressing for green salads, as well as the cabbage-carrot slaw above.

    3 tablespoons olive oil
    2 tablespoons cider vinegar
    1 tablespoon Dijon mustard
    1 tablespoon honey
    1/2 teaspoon dried savory
    1 teaspoon tamari (or to taste)

Whisk the ingredients together. Use immediately, or keep refrigerated.

Desserts

FLICKER WARS

Everyone who has ever had a cabin in the woods knows that nature and its inhabitants do not always cooperate with the goals of man. Thatch ants can march up the driveway and set up camp right next to your new shop building. A porcupine can spend a few days munching on the top of an old, forked tree and then without warning kill your favorite sapling by girdling it at porcupine-shoulder height.

Flickers, woodpeckers which like to nest in large trees, had never bothered our house much before. This year they wouldn't take no for an answer. As I sat at my computer in the early mornings, cup of herb tea in hand, I would hear a ck-click as a flicker landed on the wall, a few tentative taps, and then a thunk-thunk as it settled down to the serious business of making a home in our wall. Each time, I ran out the door, clapping my hands and following the flicker until it flew away. This scene was repeated every morning until we had to leave for Lance's family reunion in Kansas.

Before we left, Lance put flash-tape up on all the places where birds had landed and pecked at the house. Flash-tape is mylar ribbon, silver on one side and colored on the other. When twisted and then attached loosely at both ends, it swirls, jiggles and flashes color and movement in the least little breath of air. We hoped that, being new, it would deter the flickers at least for the length of our trip.

It wasn't enough. When we arrived home 10 days later, we found a three-inch-diameter hole in the west end of the house (right under a "V" of flash tape). The adjacent lawn was covered with bits of wood and shredded insulation. The mess would take days to clean up.

Now, we love all our native birds, and try to encourage them to live here. Woodpeckers eat **lots** of insects. Sometimes I wake up on summer mornings and see a flicker sitting on the ground at the edge of the lawn, poking at an anthill and eating everything that comes out of it. I admire that persistence, and benefit from it, unless it is exercised against my house!

One day I became aware of rustling noises in the house. At first, I assumed the noise I heard was nearby but outside. Then I walked over to see if there was perhaps a mouse or even a tree frog (as had happened before) behind the stove. The rustling came again. It was **inside** the stove! I called to Lance that there might possibly be a bird in the stove, envisioning a chickadee fallen down the chimney. I opened the lid, and out flew a flicker!!! This way and that, it flew across the ceiling leaving sooty wing-marks and hiding in the spider plant, until finally it took aim at the open door and glided out. We heard a mournful "cheer" from the pine woods.

Lance and I looked at each other and burst out laughing. The flicker had found the largest opening in the house and tried to enter that way. It must not have been a rewarding experience, because it hasn't come near the house since (but there's a little hole in the end of the shed...).

....from "Morning Hill News" #41 May/June '98

40

INTRODUCTION TO THE SOLAR BAKERY

LOAVES, such as breads and cakes, do not have as much moisture in them as a casserole and they will come up to temperature much more quickly. You must put them in a preheated cooker because rising dough must be cooked or it will fall again. Watch your preheating cooker carefully, because an empty solar cooker will quickly get hot enough to smoke the finish off the inside. It is the mass of food inside which controls the temperature. A small jar of water will be enough to moderate the temperature in a preheating oven. A rock or brick placed to heat in the empty cooker will provide mass to help hold the heat whenever you open the door to put food in, and it will help provide bottom heat to your baked goods.

⚙

TEMPERATURE: Put an **oven thermometer** in your solar cooker where you can see it without opening the door. Preheat the cooker to 300-400 degrees. Being precise isn't necessary because as soon as you put your loaf or cake in the oven, the temperature will fall to 300 degrees or less. Don't worry; quick breads and cakes will cook JUST FINE. Turn the cooker as frequently as you can to keep it facing into the sun. **Cooking time** may only be about 15 to 20 percent longer than in a conventional oven. When your bread or cake looks done, open the cooker and check it. If it isn't quite, then five minutes more will usually do the job.

HOW MUCH TO BAKE AT ONE TIME: This is one time when you absolutely cannot put more food in the cooker and have it bake properly (unless you have a large one). Two loaves of bread are too much for most cookers! One standard loaf will usually do just fine, and remember: even if the sun goes behind a cloud, and your loaf turns out flat-topped, it will still taste just as good!

✴

BAKING PANS: I use dark-coated tin pans for baking breads and cakes. If the pan doesn't fit in your cooker one way, turn it a quarter-turn and try it another way. Make sure the pan fits and the cooker is set up for it before getting the cooker preheated and the dough or batter in the pan. Your graniteware may also be used as a baking pan.

BLUE RIBBON GINGERBREAD

A moist, gingery cake that is spiced just right. Use dark, or blackstrap molasses for best flavor. Yes, this gingerbread won a blue ribbon at the county fair!

Makes an 8X8-inch cake:

    12/3 cups whole wheat pastry flour
    11/4 teaspoons baking soda
    11/4 teaspoons ginger
    1 teaspoon cinnamon
    1/4 teaspoon ground cloves
    1/3 cup oil
    1/2 cup honey
    1/4 cup dark molasses
    1 egg
    3/4 cup boiling water

Preheat the solar cooker with 1 cup of water in it. Bring the water to a boil, and have ready for the recipe. Lightly oil an 8X8-inch square cake pan.

Sift together the flour, soda, ginger, cinnamon and cloves into a medium bowl. Spoon the mixture back into the sifter. Measure the oil, honey and molasses into the bowl. Add the egg. Beat with a mixer until frothy. Sift the dry ingredients into the wet mixture in 3 parts, beating well after each addition. The batter will get very stiff with the third addition (if you are using a hand rotary beater, you may have to finish this with a spoon).

Add the boiling water, and beat with a mixer or rotary beater for a full minute. The batter will be thin. Pour the batter into the prepared pan, and bake in solar cooker until the cake tests done. Cool 10 minutes in the pan, then cut into slices and remove to a rack to finish cooling.

Conventional kitchen instructions: Prepare as above. Bake for about 45 minutes in a preheated 325-degree oven until the cake tests done.

CHOCOLATE CAKE

A great classic chocolate cake: moist, heavy, almost gooey. A cake-and-ice cream cake.

Makes an 8X8-inch cake:

1 cup whole wheat pastry flour
1/3 cup unsweetened cocoa powder
1/2 teaspoon baking powder
3/4 teaspoon baking soda
3 tablespoons buttermilk powder
1/4 cup oil
1/2 cup honey
1 egg
1 teaspoon vanilla
3/4 cup boiling water

Preheat the solar cooker with 1 cup of water in it. Bring the water to the boil, and have ready for the recipe. Lightly oil an 8X8-inch square cake pan.

Set your sifter on a plate. Measure the flour, cocoa powder, baking powder, soda and buttermilk powder into it, and set aside. In a medium bowl, beat the oil, honey, egg and vanilla together until frothy. Sift in the dry ingredients in three parts, beating each well until blended (be sure to use any bran left in the sifter and any flour that fell on the plate). If you are using a hand rotary beater, you may have to finish this with a spoon.

Add the boiling water, and beat with a mixer or rotary beater for a full minute. The batter will be thin. Pour the batter into the prepared pan, and bake in solar cooker until the cake tests done. Cool in the pan, then cut into slices and remove with a spatula.

❀

Conventional kitchen instructions: Prepare as above. Bake in a preheated 325-degree oven for 30 to 35 minutes, until the cake tests done.

MADELYN'S MAPLE-FILBERT CAKE

This cake was created for a friend in Idaho.

Makes one 8X8-inch cake of 12 pieces:

    1 cup whole wheat pastry flour
    3/4 cup ground filbert or hazelnut meal*
    11/2 teaspoons baking powder
    1/2 teaspoon baking soda
    1/4 cup non-instant dry milk powder
    1/3 cup oil
    1/2 teaspoon vanilla
    1/2 cup dark maple syrup
    1 egg
    1/2 cup boiling water

Preheat your solar cooker with 1 cup of water in it. Bring the water to the boil, and keep it ready for the recipe. Lightly oil an 8X8-inch square cake pan, and line it with bakers paper if you wish.

In a medium bowl, stir together the flour, ground nut meal*, baking powder, soda and milk powder. Set aside. In a large bowl, beat together the oil, vanilla, maple syrup and egg. Add the dry mixture to the wet in three installments, beating well after each one (if you are using a hand rotary beater, you may have to stir the last one in with a spoon). Add the boiling water, and beat at high speed for one full minute.

Pour the batter into the prepared pan, and bake in the solar cooker until the cake tests done. Cool 10 minutes in the pan, then remove whole (if you have used bakers paper), or cut into 12 slices and remove with a spatula to a rack to cool. This is a very moist and tender cake.

Conventional kitchen instructions: Prepare as above. Bake in a preheated 350-degree oven for 30 to 35 minutes, until the cake tests done.

* To grind hazelnuts: Measure out the amount you need of whole nuts. Pulse them in the blender or food processor until finely ground, not worrying about small pieces that remain. Do not grind too much or you will have nut butter. If you wish to skin the nuts first, you may toast them for 10 minutes in a solar cooker or 350-degree oven, and then rub the skins off, but it is not necessary (although it will give the cake a finer flavor). Measure again after grinding.

BUTTERMILK SPICE CAKE

I have a friend who used to bring a piece of this cake in every single one of his sack lunches, and I just had to ask for the recipe. Of course, it's a little different now...

Makes an 8X8-inch cake of 12 pieces:

  11/4 cups whole wheat pastry flour
  1 teaspoon baking soda
  1/2 teaspoon cinnamon
  1/2 teaspoon allspice
  1/4 teaspoon grated nutmeg
  1/4 cup buttermilk powder
  1/3 cup oil
  1/2 cup honey
  1 egg
  3/4 cup boiling water
  1/3 cup coarsely chopped walnuts

Preheat the solar cooker with 1 cup of water in it. Bring the water to a boil, and have ready for the recipe. Lightly oil an 8X8-inch square cake pan, and line it with bakers paper if you wish.

Sift together the flour, soda, baking powder, cinnamon, allspice, and buttermilk powder. Put the mixture back into the sifter and set aside. In a medium bowl, beat together the oil, honey and egg until very frothy. Sift in the flour mixture in 4 installments, beating well after each (if you are using a hand rotary beater, you may have to stir the last one in with a spoon). Add the boiling water and beat for 1 minute. Fold in the chopped nuts, and pour the mixture into the prepared pan.

Bake until the cake tests done. Remove the cake whole (if you have used the paper), or cool in the pan 10 minutes, then cut into 12 pieces and remove to a rack to cool. Cool thoroughly before storing in an airtight container in a cool place.

⊕

Conventional kitchen instructions: Bake in a preheated 350-degree oven for 40 to 45 minutes.

APPLE-HAZELNUT TORTE

A simple-to-make nut torte, best eaten the day it is made.

Makes an 8-inch round torte (6-8 slices):
- 2/3 cup ground hazelnut meal*
- 1/4 cup oil
- 1/2 cup honey
- 2 eggs
- 1/2 teaspoon vanilla
- 3/4 cup whole wheat pastry flour
- 1 teaspoon baking powder
- 2 medium apples, peeled and sliced 1/4-inch thick

Topping:
- 1 tablespoon oil
- 1 tablespoon honey
- 1/2 teaspoon cinnamon

Set the solar cooker out to preheat. Prepare an 8-inch round springform pan by oiling the sides and lining the bottom with baker's paper.

In a medium bowl, combine the ground hazelnut meal*, oil, honey, eggs and vanilla. Beat well with a rotary beater until frothy. Add the flour and baking powder and continue beating until the batter is light and fluffy. Pour the batter into the springform pan.

Arrange the apple slices on the batter (they don't have to be neat -- it will rise up over them). In a very small cup, combine the oil, honey and cinnamon for the topping. Warm it in the solar cooker just enough to combine. Spoon it over the top of the torte, drizzling it over all the apples.

Bake the torte in a preheated solar cooker until the batter puffs up around the apples and is well-browned and set-up. Cool on a rack for 10 minutes before running a knife around the edges and removing the sides of the pan. Serve warm or at room temperature.

Conventional kitchen instructions: Assemble as above, using stove or microwave to warm the honey topping. Bake for 45 to 55 minutes in a preheated 350-degree oven. Cool as above.

* To grind hazelnuts: Measure out the amount you need of whole nuts. Pulse them in the blender or food processor until finely ground, not worrying about small pieces that remain. Do not grind too much or you will have nut butter. If you wish to skin the nuts first, you may toast them for 10 minutes in a solar cooker or 350-degree oven, and then rub the skins off, but it is not necessary (although it will give the torte a finer flavor). Measure again after grinding.

PEACH PUDDING CAKE

This is a moist, sweet cake over a thick sauce full of peach chunks. Keep the peaches at room temperature. Make sure you heat the sauce ingredients well. If you do not, the sauce will be too cold and won't bubble and thicken properly.

Serves 6:

31/2 cups peaches, peeled and diced (about 4 medium peaches)
11/3 cups whole wheat pastry flour
2 teaspoons baking powder
1/2 teaspoon cinnamon
3/4 cup milk
2 tablespoons oil
1/4 cup honey

Sauce:
1 tablespoon rum
1/3 cup honey
3/4 cup water
1/4 teaspoon almond extract
1 tablespoon fresh lemon juice

Set your solar cooker out to preheat with the sauce ingredients in a one-pint canning jar (screw the lid on **loosely**), and let them come to a boil. Get out a 2-liter or larger baking dish.

Place the diced peaches in the bottom of the baking dish. In a medium bowl, stir together the flour, baking powder and cinnamon. In a measuring cup or small bowl, stir together the milk, oil and honey until well blended. Add the liquid to the dry mixture, stir together well, and pour over the peaches (don't worry about spreading it out evenly).

Pour the boiling sauce liquid over the batter and apples, but **do not stir**. It will sink down through the batter into the apples. Put the dish immediately into the solar cooker, uncovered, and bake until the cake top is golden and done **and** you can see the sauce bubbling up and thickening around the edges.

Serve hot, with the sauce spooned over the cake.

❁

Conventional kitchen instructions: Heat the sauce ingredients to boiling in a small saucepan over medium heat. Bake in a preheated 350-degree oven for 45 to 50 minutes, until the cake is golden on top and the sauce has begun to bubble up around the sides.

STRAWBERRY THREE-CHEESE CAKE

This is the world's best low-fat cheesecake. It's well worth the trouble of having all three cheeses on hand. You need a blender to make a smooth, creamy filling.

Makes an 8-inch round cake of 8 small pieces:

Crust:
>   3/4 cup graham cracker crumbs
>   2 tablespoons oil
>   2 tablespoons honey

Filling:
>   2/3 cup Ricotta cheese
>   2/3 cup cottage cheese
>   3 egg yolks
>   1 tablespoon lemon juice
>   1/2 teaspoon vanilla
>   1/2 teaspoon lemon peel
>   1 tablespoon whole wheat pastry flour
>   6 ounces Neufchâtel cheese
>   3 egg whites
>   1/4 cup honey

Set your solar cooker out to preheat. Prepare an 8-inch round springform pan by oiling it lightly.

Blend the crust ingredients together in a bowl with a fork. Press the crust into the bottom of the pan, and 1/2 inch up the sides. Bake in the solar cooker until it begins to darken, only 5 to 10 minutes.

Blend the Ricotta and cottage cheese in an electric blender on high speed until smooth and liquid, stopping the blender frequently to push the cheeses down onto the blades with a rubber spatula. Add the egg yolks, lemon juice, vanilla, lemon peel and flour. Blend again until smooth. Blend in the Neufchâtel cheese.

In a medium bowl, beat the egg whites with clean beaters until they hold a soft peak. Beat in the honey. Pour the cheese mixture from the blender, and fold it into the egg whites. Pour the mixture over the crust in the springform pan.

Bake in the solar cooker until the cheese mixture is fully set, and golden on top. This must be chilled if it is to be kept more than 6 hours, but it tastes best if served at room temperature. Serve with fresh strawberry sauce.

FRESH STRAWBERRY SAUCE

Use either fresh or frozen strawberries for this. I freeze home-grown strawberries mashed, so they won't freezer-burn. Then I make cheesecake topping, or just thaw them and put them straight on vanilla ice cream!

11/2 cups partially mashed strawberries
1 tablespoon honey (optional)
2 tablespoons arrowroot

Combine all ingredients in a pint canning jar, put the lid on loosely, and cook in your solar cooker until the sauce bubbles and thickens. Remove, spread on top of the cheesecake, and cool.

❁

Conventional kitchen instructions: Assemble crust and filling as above. Bake the crust in a preheated 350-degree oven about 10 minutes, until it firms up and begins to darken. Bake the cake at 325 degrees for about 1 hour, until filling is set and golden on top. Cook the strawberry sauce in a small pan over medium heat, stirring frequently, until it bubbles and thickens.

STRAWBERRY-RHUBARB COBBLER

Strawberries and rhubarb just seem to go together naturally. The sweetness of the strawberries offsets the tartness of the rhubarb, and if you have both in your garden, the berries ripen about the time the rhubarb is standing tall.

Makes 6 generous servings:

    1 dry pint strawberries (11/2 cups prepared berries)
    11/2 pounds rhubarb (3 cups prepared rhubarb)
    1 tablespoon arrowroot
    1/2 cup honey
    1/8 teaspoon ground cloves
    1/2 teaspoon orange peel

Cake:
    11/2 cups whole wheat pastry flour
    1 teaspoon baking powder
    1/2 teaspoon baking soda
    1 Tablespoon buttermilk powder
    1/4 teaspoon cinnamon
    3 tablespoons oil
    1/4 cup honey
    1 teaspoon vanilla
    1 egg
    2/3 cup milk

Clean and crush or slice the strawberries. You should have about 11/2 cups. Wash and slice 3 cups rhubarb. Combine the fruit in a 2-liter or larger casserole, and sprinkle the arrowroot over it to dissolve. Add the honey, cloves and orange peel, and mix thoroughly. Cover, and place in solar cooker until the sauce bubbles and thickens.

While the sauce is heating, make the cake. Sift together the pastry flour, baking powder, soda, buttermilk powder, and cinnamon into a medium bowl. In a separate medium bowl, beat together the oil, honey, vanilla, eggs and milk. Add the dry mixture in 4 portions, beating each time until well blended.

Remove the casserole from the solar cooker. Scrape the cake batter over the thickened sauce, distributing evenly. Replace in the cooker uncovered, and bake until the cake is golden and springy to the touch, with the sauce bubbling up around it.

Serve warm, with the sauce spooned over the cake.

Conventional kitchen instructions: Cook the sauce in a large saucepan over medium-low heat, stirring frequently, until thick. Do not heat it too fast, or it will stick. Scrape the sauce into a casserole as above, or a 9X9-inch nonreactive pan. Bake in a preheated 375-degree oven for 30 minutes, until the cake is golden and the sauce bubbles up around it.

☼

APPLE BROWN BETTY

A classic dessert from New England, its simplicity is deceptive: you could grow addicted to this one. Make it in your covered casserole to keep the crumbs from drying out, then remove the lid to brown them.

Serves 4-6:
    2 cups wholegrain bread crumbs
    1/4 cup butter or 3 tablespoons oil
    6 cups sliced apples
    1/4 cup honey
    1/4 teaspoon grated nutmeg
    21/2 tablespoons fresh lemon juice
    1/2 cup hot water

Preheat solar cooker and lightly oil a 2-liter casserole. Put a small saucepan in the cooker with the butter or oil to melt. Mix crumbs and butter or oil lightly with fork. Cover bottom of casserole with 1/3 of the crumbs. Spread 1/2 the apples over the crumbs. In a small cup, mix together the honey, nutmeg and lemon juice. Drizzle 1/2 the honey mixture over the apples.

Repeat the layers with another 1/3 of the crumbs, the rest of the apples, and honey mixture. Top with the remaining crumbs and drizzle the hot water over all.

Bake, covered, until simmering. Remove the cover and continue baking until the apples are tender and the crumbs turn golden.

Serve warm with whipped cream or ice cream.

Conventional kitchen instructions: Preheat the oven to 350 degrees. Melt the butter or warm the oil in a small saucepan, and stir in the crumbs. Assemble the dish as above. Bake, covered, for 25 minutes, then remove the cover and bake for another 20 to 25 minutes, until the apples are tender and the crumbs turn golden.

HONEY APPLE CRISP

A classic; moist, sweet apples with a crunchy oat topping.

Serves 6-8:

> 6-8 medium apples
> 2 tablespoons quick-cooking tapioca
> 1/3 cup honey
> 1 tablespoon lemon juice

Topping:
> 1/4 cup honey
> 2 tablespoons oil
> 1/2 teaspoon vanilla
> 1 cup regular rolled oats
> 1/4 cup whole wheat flour
> 1/2 cup chopped walnuts

Start the topping first. Set your solar cooker out to preheat, with the oil and honey in a small heatproof bowl in it. When it is warm (do not let it boil), remove it and stir in the vanilla, then add the oats and toss with a fork till they are well-coated. Set aside.

Get out a 2-liter or larger casserole. Wash, quarter and core the apples, then slice them finely. You should have 6-7 cups of apple (exact amount is not critical).

Sprinkle 1 tablespoon of the tapioca over the bottom of the casserole, add half the apples, and repeat, using the rest of the tapioca and apples. Blend the 1/3 cup honey and the lemon juice together, and drizzle it over the apples. Cover the casserole, and bake 35 to 40 minutes or until the liquid in the apples begins to bubble.

Finish mixing the topping. Add the flour and walnuts, and mix well. When the apples boil, remove the casserole from the cooker and crumble the topping over the apples. Bake, uncovered, until the topping is golden and the juice bubbles all around it. Apple crisp is best served warm.

⊕

Conventional kitchen instructions: Warm and mix your topping ingredients in a small saucepan over low heat. Do not boil. Mix as above, and do the baking in a preheated 325-degree oven.

SQUASH PIE

Squash pie is quite similar to pumpkin pie, but smoother and richer. Of course, you may make this pie with pumpkin as well, but try the squash! You may prefer it.

Makes a 10-inch pie:

Pastry for a single **crust**

Filling:
1 1/4 cups water or squash cooking liquid
1/2 cup milk powder
1/3 cup honey
1 teaspoon cinnamon
1/2 teaspoon ginger
1/8 teaspoon nutmeg
2 eggs
1 3/4 cups cooked, mashed squash or pumpkin

Prepare the pie crust dough and line the pie plate with it. In a blender or bowl, combine all the ingredients except the squash. Beat or blend thoroughly. Add the squash in several batches, beating or blending each time until thoroughly incorporated.

Pour the filling into the crust. Bake in a preheated solar cooker until the filling sets up and a knife inserted in the filling comes out clean. Cool to room temperature, or chill before serving.

Conventional kitchen instructions: Bake the pie in a preheated 350-degree oven for 50 to 60 minutes, until the pie tests done.

Hint: If your crust comes out soggy, it may not be getting enough bottom heat to cook with the filling in it. Cook it first for 15 to 20 minutes empty, or lined with foil weighted down with some dry beans. Then add the pie filling and finish baking the pie.

CHOCOLATE-MINT RICOTTA MOUSSE

A velvety-smooth mousse with a secret!

Serves 6:
    21/2 squares unsweetened chocolate
    1/2 cup honey
    1 15-ounce container low-fat Ricotta cheese
    1/4 cup spearmint leaves, packed

Measure the honey in a heat-proof cup. Break up the chocolate squares and add them to the honey, pushing the chocolate down so it is covered. Heat honey and chocolate in the solar cooker just until the chocolate melts.
Scrape the honey and chocolate into a blender. Add the Ricotta cheese and mint leaves. Blend until liquid and smooth. You may have to stop the blender frequently and scrape down the sides with a rubber spatula, pushing the cheese down onto the blender blades.
When smooth, pour into a serving dish or individual cups. Chill for at least two hours before serving. Garnish with fresh mint leaves.

Conventional kitchen instructions: Melt the chocolate and honey together over the lowest possible heat or a double boiler, just until the chocolate is melted enough to blend into the honey. Proceed as above.

HOT FUDGE SAUCE

For ice cream or desserts. Sinfully rich-tasting.

Makes 2 servings:
    1/4 cup honey
    2 tablespoons cocoa powder
    1/4 teaspoon almond or vanilla extract

Blend the cocoa powder and honey. Heat in solar cooker in an uncovered dish until the cocoa powder turns dark and melts. Remove from cooker, stir in the extract. Use immediately as a hot fudge, or cool and use later (it will be **very** thick if you cool it).
Recipe may be multiplied for more servings.

Conventional kitchen instructions: Warm the honey and cocoa very gently over the lowest possible heat just until the cocoa melts and can be stirred into the honey.

Snacking Cakes
Quick Breads & Muffins
Breakfasts

VOLUNTEERING

In a small community like Grant County (pop. about 8,000), anyone who is active in any kind of public capacity gets to be known. You don't have to try to be a public person, you just have to do the things you like to do.

I collared a county candidate in the post office before an election and asked him for his opinion about an issue, and the following summer he approached me after he spoke at the Prairie City Earth Day celebration. He wanted to know if I would be willing to volunteer to coordinate a Household Hazardous Waste Collection Event for the county. I really liked the idea of doing something concrete to improve the quality of life where I live.

Filling out the application was easy. All I had to do was write a two-page essay about what I thought I was going to do, and send it in. Once the DEQ accepted the application, the real work began. The DEQ brings in a contractor who actually handles all the waste and removes it from the community. My job was to make sure everyone knew that they were coming, and to provide a few volunteers to direct traffic and handle peripheral duties.

I've been busy as a beaver for the last four months, writing press releases to keep some copy in the paper about it almost every week. I begged a friend who is a graphic artist to design a poster for us, and she came up with a picture of a cowboy on a "paint" horse, lassoing a clutter of paint and solvent cans. The caption reads "Round Up Your Old Paint."

I went to the grade school and the Education Service District to beg them to make the poster available to teachers who might like to have their classes color them, and then I returned to pick up the finished posters and put them around town. As I taped the posters in shop windows, I admired the creative work. Every one was different. There were artistic shadings, polka-dots, all colors of horses, and all colors of cowboy hats.

There hadn't been a hazardous waste collection in our county since before the DEQ records began. People had basements full of old paint cans, many of which undoubtedly contained lead. I was asked about disposal of freon, Draino, batteries, dirty solvents, and a host of other things. Sometimes I had to go and phone the DEQ office for help, and get back to the questioner. I've been learning a lot about hazardous materials. I learned about several of the hazardous materials I had naively used in my past. Oh, my, the things we all expose ourselves to in our ignorance!

The big day was April 5th. People began lining up almost an hour before the posted time to begin. Based on population estimates, the DEQ figured we'd have 90 households turn out. By 11:30 a.m., 90 had come and they were still lining up. The final total was 152. By 5 p.m., the parking lot was empty and the waste hauled away.

My goal was to have no one say "I didn't bring my stuff down because I didn't know it was happening." It seems to have worked. And, just incidentally, I seem to have made a lot of new friends.

...from the "Morning Hill News" #35, May/June '97

PINEAPPLE-COCONUT CAKE

Makes a great snacking cake, or serve warm for a dessert.

Makes a 9X9-inch cake of 12 pieces:

    2 cups whole wheat pastry flour
    1 teaspoon baking powder
    1 teaspoon baking soda
    1 tablespoon buttermilk powder
    1/4 teaspoon nutmeg
    1 egg
    1/2 cup oil
    2/3 cup honey
    2/3 cup yogurt
    1 cup crushed pineapple
    1/2 cup unsweetened coconut
    1 tablespoon lemon juice

Set your solar cooker out to preheat. Lightly oil a 9X9-inch square cake pan, and line it with bakers paper if you wish.

Sift together the flour, baking powder, soda, buttermilk powder and nutmeg. In a large bowl, stir together the egg, oil, honey, yogurt, crushed pineapple, coconut and lemon juice until thoroughly mixed. Add the dry mixture to the wet mixture in 3 or 4 installments, beating with a spoon until well-mixed each time. Scrape the batter into the prepared pan.

Bake in the solar cooker until the cake tests done. Let cool 5 minutes in pan, then remove from pan and cool on a wire rack. May be served warm or at room temperature.

Conventional kitchen instructions: Prepare as above. Bake in a preheated 350-degree oven for 30 to 40 minutes, until the cake tests done.

RHUBARB BUTTERMILK CAKE

Rhubarb needs no added moisture to make a cake, so to get great flavor, I use powdered buttermilk (available at health food stores or in the powdered milk section of the grocery).

Makes one 8X8-inch cake of 16 pieces:

   1/3 cup finely chopped walnuts
   11/3 cups whole wheat pastry flour
   1/2 teaspoon baking soda
   1/4 cup buttermilk powder
   3 cups diced rhubarb
   1 egg
   1 tablespoon oil
   1/3 cup honey
   1 teaspoon vanilla

Preheat the solar cooker and lightly oil an 8X8-inch square cake pan. Sprinkle about half the chopped nuts over the bottom of the pan, and set aside.

Measure the flour, baking soda and buttermilk powder into a medium bowl. Stir until well blended. Dice the rhubarb 1/4 to 1/2-inch (to your taste, it does not need to be perfectly regular). Toss the rhubarb with the dry ingredients and set aside.

Measure 1/3 cup honey, and add the oil, egg and vanilla to it right in the measuring cup. Stir together well, then scrape it out over the rhubarb mixture. Toss and stir until ingredients are thoroughly moistened. The mixture will be stiff.

Spoon the mixture into the pan, being careful to distribute evenly over the nuts without disturbing them. Push down and smooth over the top. Sprinkle the remaining nuts over the top, and bake in solar cooker until the cake tests done.

Let rest in the pan 10 minutes to cool, then slice into 16 pieces and remove the pieces to a rack with a spatula. Serve warm, or let cool thoroughly and then store in an airtight container. This resists becoming soggy, but it is best eaten the first or second day (refrigerate after the first day).

❖

Conventional kitchen instructions: Bake in a preheated 350-degree oven for 35 to 40 minutes, until the cake tests done.

LEMON MUFFINS

In Europe, the rind of conventionally grown citrus fruit from the U.S. is marked "not for consumption" because of all the pesticides that are used on it. Please use organic lemons, or leave the rind out.

Makes 12 muffins:

11/4 cups rolled oats
1/2 cup yogurt or buttermilk
Grated rind of 1 lemon
1/4 cup lemon juice
3 tablespoons oil
1/3 cup honey
1 egg
11/3 cups whole wheat bread flour
1 teaspoon baking powder
1 teaspoon baking soda

In a medium bowl, set the oats, yogurt or buttermilk, and lemon rind to soak for 15 minutes.

Set your solar cooker out to preheat. Prepare a regular muffin tin by oiling it or by lining the cups with muffin papers.

To the oat mixture, add the lemon juice, oil, honey and egg. Beat well. In a small bowl, stir together the flour, baking powder and soda until well-blended. Stir the flour mixture into the oat mixture, just to combine. Do not over-mix. Spoon the batter into the muffin tin.

Bake in solar cooker until the muffins are golden on top and test done. Let rest 5 minutes before removing from pan. Serve warm, or cool on a rack and store in an airtight place.

Conventional kitchen instructions: Bake in a preheated 400-degree oven for 18 to 20 minutes, or until the muffins test done.

FRUIT-OAT-NUT MUFFINS

The buttermilk powder adds tang and tenderness to these substantial muffins. Use of bread four allows them to withstand a lunchbox without falling apart, making them a good travel snack, too!

Makes 12 muffins:

1 1/4 cups regular rolled oats
1 1/4 cups hot water
1/2 teaspoon grated orange peel (dry or fresh, organic)
1 cup bread flour
1 1/2 teaspoons baking powder
1/2 teaspoon baking soda
1/2 teaspoon cinnamon
4 tablespoons buttermilk powder
1/2 cup raisins
1/4 cup sunflower seed
1 egg
1/4 cup honey
3 tablespoons oil

Set your solar cooker out to preheat. Prepare a regular muffin tin by oiling it or by lining the cups with muffin papers.

In a large bowl, stir together the oats, hot water (hot tap water will do fine. The hotter the water, the more tender the oats will become), and orange peel. Set aside to soak for 15 minutes.

In a medium bowl, stir together the flour, baking powder, soda, cinnamon and buttermilk powder. When thoroughly blended, stir in the raisins and sunflower seed.

Beat the egg, honey and oil into the wet oat mixture. Stir in the dry ingredients, and mix just to combine. Spoon the batter into the muffin tin.

Bake in the preheated cooker until the muffins test done. Let rest 5 minutes before removing from pan. Serve warm, or cool on a rack and store in an airtight place for up to 4 days.

✿

Conventional kitchen instructions: Bake in a preheated 400-degree oven for 17 to 19 minutes, or until the muffins test done.

BUTTERMILK DATE-NUT MUFFINS

Buttermilk powder and dates make these muffins tender and moist.

Makes 12 muffins:

2 1/4 cups whole wheat pastry flour
3/4 teaspoon baking soda
4 tablespoons buttermilk powder
3/4 cups date pieces
1/2 cup chopped walnuts
1 egg, beaten
2 tablespoons oil
1/4 cup honey
1 1/4 cups water

Set your solar cooker out to preheat. Prepare a regular muffin tin by oiling it or by lining the cups with muffin papers.

In a medium bowl, stir together the flour, soda and buttermilk powder. When thoroughly blended, stir in the date pieces and chopped nuts. In a separate bowl, beat the egg, oil, honey and water. Stir in the dry ingredients, and mix just to combine. Spoon the batter into the muffin tin.

Bake in the solar cooker until the muffins are golden on top and test done. Let rest on rack 5 minutes before removing from pan. Serve warm, or cool on a rack and store in an airtight place.

⊕

Conventional kitchen instructions: Bake in a preheated 400-degree oven for 17 to 19 minutes, or until the muffins test done.

FRESH APPLE BREAD

This sweet and tender quickbread goes wonderfully in a lunchbox. Use all-purpose whole wheat flour, or a 50-50 blend of bread and pastry flour. If you prefer muffins, this recipe will make a dozeh regular muffins.

Makes a 5X9-inch loaf:

2 cups whole wheat flour (see above)
1 teaspoon baking powder
1 teaspoon baking soda
1 teaspoon cinnamon
11/2 cups finely chopped apple
1/2 cup chopped walnuts
1/4 cup oil
1/2 cup honey
1 egg
1/2 cup milk

Set your solar cooker out to preheat. Prepare a 5X9-inch loaf pan by oiling it lightly.

Sift the flour, baking powder, soda and cinnamon together into a medium bowl. Add the chopped apples and nuts, and toss to coat. In a small bowl, whisk together the oil, honey, egg and milk. Add the wet ingredients to the dry and stir just until all ingredients are moistened. Do not worry about any small lumps.

Bake in the solar cooker until the loaf is golden on top and tests done. Cool 10 minutes in the pan before removing to a rack to finish cooling. This loaf is best stored in the refrigerator, because of the moistness of the apples.

Conventional kitchen instructions: Bake in a preheated 350-degree oven for 50 to 60 minutes, or until the loaf tests done. If the top browns too quickly, put a foil cap over the loaf or put a cookie sheet on the shelf above it.

BUTTERMILK BISCUITS

Moist, tender, light and tasty. I like the powdered buttermilk because it is always on the shelf, but you may substitute 11/3 cups fresh buttermilk for the powder and water.

Makes 10 3-inch biscuits:

> 2 cups whole wheat pastry flour
> 1/2 cup fine whole wheat bread flour
> 1/4 teaspoon salt
> 21/2 teaspoons baking powder
> 1/2 teaspoon baking soda
> 1/4 cup buttermilk powder
> 11/4 cup water
> 1 tablespoon oil

Preheat your solar cooker. Get out a 9X13-inch baking sheet.

In a medium bowl, stir together the flours, salt, baking powder, soda and buttermilk powder until well-blended. In a 2-cup measuring cup or small bowl, add the oil to the water. Stirring the oil and water together with a fork, pour them over the dry mixture. Now stir the liquid into the flour with the fork.

Note about biscuits in general: For the most tender biscuits, it is best to have a dough that is **almost** too soft to work with your hands. Everyone's flour and climate are different. If your flour is dry, it is best to start with a little less pastry flour and have to add a little more flour after the liquid to make your dough firm enough to handle. With practice, you will discover what is the correct amount of flour for the recipe. If your dough is too soft, merely sprinkle a little more pastry flour over it and stir it in until you reach the right consistency.

Turn the dough out onto a floured board and knead 6 to 8 times, just enough to make it come together. Roll or pat out the dough 3/4-inch thick. Use a cutter or thin-edged drinking glass to cut out the biscuits. Place them on the ungreased cookie sheet and bake until light golden on top.

✧

Conventional kitchen instructions: Bake in a preheated 425-degree oven for 12 to 14 minutes, until done.

Yes! You can make hot tea, coffee, and other drinks in your solar cooker! Boil a container of water for your morning cup of java, or try the mixtures here, heated in a canning jar with a perforated lid:

GIN-ZING TEA
A good energizer for midmorning.

Makes 1 mugful:
2 slices fresh gingerroot
1 slice fresh lemon
1 cup boiling water
1 capsule powdered ginseng root
1 heaping spoonful of honey (to taste)

Put the gingerroot in a mug, and squeeze the lemon slice over it (if it is an organic lemon, drop the rind in too). Cover with boiling water. Steep 5 minutes. Remove the chunks, stir in the contents of the ginseng capsule, and sweeten to taste.

HOT CHOCOLATE

Makes 2 mugs full:
2 cups milk
11/2 tablespoons unsweetened cocoa powder
1/4 teaspoon vanilla
2 tablespoons honey (or to taste)

Combine all ingredients in a 1-quart jar. Heat in solar cooker until steaming, but **do not boil**. Whisk the melted cocoa powder into the milk. Pour into mugs and enjoy.
Variations: substitute almond extract for the vanilla, or add a tablespoon of any fruit or nut liqueur after removing from cooker.

HOT ALMOND MILK
A soothing alternative for non-chocolate lovers (are there any?)

Makes 2 mugs full:
2 cups milk
3/4 teaspoon almond extract
2 tablespoons honey (or to taste)
Pinch of cinnamon

Combine all ingredients in a jar, and heat until steaming.

Conventional kitchen instructions: Follow procedures outlined above, using a 1-quart saucepan over medium heat to make your beverage. Pour into mugs and enjoy.

RASPBERRY SEVEN-GRAIN CAKE

You might have to wait till next summer to make this with fresh raspberries. Meanwhile, try some frozen ones, or dice up some juicy peaches, and make it Peach Cake.

Makes an 8X8-inch cake of 12 pieces:

Topping: 1/2 tablespoon oil
        1 tablespoon honey
        1/4 teaspoon cinnamon

Cake: 1/3 cup seven-grain cereal
        1/2 cup yogurt
        1 1/4 cups whole wheat pastry flour
        1/2 teaspoon baking soda
        1 teaspoon baking powder
        1/4 teaspoon dry, grated orange or lemon peel
        1/2 teaspoon cinnamon
        1/4 cup oil
        1/3 cup honey
        1 egg
        1 tablespoon lemon juice
        1 teaspoon vanilla
        1 cup raspberries, fresh or frozen

Set your solar cooker out to preheat. Lightly oil an 8X8-inch square cake pan. Put the topping ingredients in a small heatproof cup, and warm in the preheating cooker just until they will blend. Do not boil.

In a medium bowl, stir the cereal and yogurt together. Let soak for 10 minutes. In a separate bowl, stir together the flour, soda, baking powder, peel and cinnamon. Set aside. Add the oil, honey, egg, lemon juice and vanilla to the yogurt mixture. Stir well to mix. Add the dry mixture to the wet mixture. Stir just to combine.

Spread the batter in the prepared pan. Spread the berries loosely over the top (the batter will puff up around them as it bakes). Stir the topping ingredients together and spoon/drizzle them over the top of the cake.

Bake in the solar cooker until done. Cut into 12 pieces while still in the pan, and remove the pieces to a rack with a spatula. Serve warm, or at room temperature. May be kept in the refrigerator for 3 to 4 days.

Conventional kitchen instructions: Warm topping ingredients on a very low burner. Prepare the cake as above. Bake in a preheated 350-degree oven for 35 to 40 minutes, or until the cake tests done.

SKILLET WAFFLE

This waffle, cooked in a solar cooker in a cast-iron skillet, looks like a big fluffy soufflé, but tastes just like Grandma's waffles. That's because it **is** my Grandma's waffle recipe. You can also make it in a waffle iron, just like she did.

Serves 4:

2 tablespoons oil for skillet
2 cups all-purpose whole wheat flour
3 teaspoons baking powder
1/4 teaspoon salt
3 eggs, separated
2 tablespoons oil
1 teaspoon honey
11/3 cups milk (more or less)

Set your solar cooker out to preheat. Put a 101/2-inch cast iron skillet in it to preheat about 10 minutes, with 2 tablespoons oil in the skillet.

Measure the flour, baking powder and salt into your sifter. Set the sifter aside on a plate. Separate the egg yolks into a large bowl, and the egg whites into a medium one. Set the whites aside. Measure the oil, honey and milk in with the egg yolks. Beat the wet mixture well with a spoon, then sift in the mixture in the sifter, adding any that fell on the plate and stirring to combine well. If batter is too thick to fold egg whites into, add a little more milk.

Look to see if your skillet is adequately preheated. A drop of water should sizzle on the oil. Swirl the oil around to coat the bottom of the pan. Keep the skillet in the cooker.

With a clean beater, whip the egg whites until stiff peaks form. Fold the egg whites into the batter. Remove the skillet from the solar cooker. Pour the batter into the skillet, and replace it quickly in the cooker. Bake until the puff is golden on the top and tests done.

Slice into wedges and serve hot, with fruit and yogurt or maple syrup.

✿

Conventional kitchen instructions: Bake in a preheated 350-degree oven for about 30 minutes, or follow the instructions for your waffle iron.

GONE-NUTS GRANOLA

This is a good, simple granola with no dried fruit in it. It goes wonderfully with whatever fruit is fresh in season.

Makes 5 cups:

1/4 cup oil
1/4 cup honey
31/2 cups old-fashioned rolled oats
1 teaspoon cinnamon
1/2 cup cashew pieces
1/2 cup walnuts
1/4 cup almonds or hazelnuts
1/4 cup sunflower seeds
1/4 cup coconut

Set your solar cooker out to preheat.
Put the honey and oil in a small heatproof cup. Warm it in the solar cooker just until it will flow and blend. **Do not boil**. In a large bowl, pour the honey mixture over the rolled oats, tossing to coat thoroughly. Then add all the other ingredients and stir well.
Pour the granola into a 9X13-inch baking pan and set it in the solar cooker. Take the pan out and stir the mixture after 10 or 15 minutes, paying attention to the corners so they do not burn. Check and stir the mixture at more frequent intervals until it turns golden and is almost dry. When it is nearly done, you may have to check it every three minutes or so. In a solar cooker, this may take quite a long time to start browning, but once heated through it will finish very fast, so watch it carefully!
Remove the granola from the cooker. Cool at room temperature, tossing frequently to insure that ingredients do not stick together. When completely cool, store in airtight containers in a cool place.

Conventional kitchen instructions: Warm the honey and oil in a large pot over a very low burner. **Do not boil.** Add the other ingredients to the honey and oil in the pot, stir well, then pour into a 9X13-inch pan. Bake in a preheated 350-degree oven, following instructions as above.

ALMOND-ORANGE GRANOLA

This granola can be altered to suit your mood, just change the type and/or proportion of sweeteners to your taste. Anyway, it's a flavorful way to start your day.

Makes about 5 1/2 cups:

    1/3 cup oil
    1/3 cup sweetener*
    4 cups rolled oats
    1/2 teaspoon almond extract
    1 teaspoon dried orange peel
    1/2 cup unsweetened flaked coconut
    1/2 cup raw sunflower seed
    2/3 cup chopped or chunked almonds
    1 cup raisins

Set your solar cooker out to preheat.

Measure the oil into a small heatproof cup, and then use the same cup to measure the sweetener* (*for sweetener, use honey, maple, molasses, barley-malt or fruit syrup to taste. My favorite combination is to fill the measure part way with honey and then add a dollop each of maple and molasses to measure a total of 1/3 cup). Warm the oil and sweetener gently in the preheating solar cooker until they will stir together. **Do not boil.**

In a large bowl, pour the honey mixture over the rolled oats, tossing to coat thoroughly. Then add all the other ingredients except the raisins and stir well. Pour the granola into a 9X13-inch baking pan and set it in the solar cooker. Take the pan out and stir the mixture after 10 or 15 minutes, paying attention to the corners so they do not burn. Check and stir the mixture at more frequent intervals until it turns golden and is almost dry. When it is nearly done, you may have to check it every three minutes or so. In a solar cooker, this may take quite a long time to start browning, but once heated through it will finish very fast, so watch it carefully!

Take the granola out of the cooker and immediately add the raisins. Stir occasionally as it cools. When completely cool, store in an airtight container in a cool place.

Conventional kitchen instructions: Warm the sweetener and oil in a large pot over a very low burner. **Do not boil.** Add the other ingredients (except raisins) to the sweetener and oil in the pot, stir well, then pour into a 9X13-inch pan. Bake in a preheated 350-degree oven, following instructions as above.

Yeast Breads

FOR MY MOM

My father called the last day of August to tell me that my mother had died. She wasn't ill, if you don't call age an illness. My sister told me afterward that Mom had been fading for a while, and she was aware of it. Her variable memory and declining physical capabilities irritated her, though, being Mom, she would never have chosen to give up. She had a will to live life to the fullest, and a vivacity and enjoyment of people that stayed with her to the last hour. While it was hard on the rest of us to lose her that suddenly, we are grateful for her that she went so simply.

Mom was in large part responsible for my interests in life. When I was a sprout of a child, she and I would bring up the rear of the family pack on hikes. "That's a Dodecatheon," Mom would say as I hunkered down in front of a Shootingstar. "Oh, Mom!" I would pout, "Just tell me the common names. I won't ever need to use Latin names." I still remember the Latin names she taught me, and hundreds more I began learning on my own when, in college, I developed an interest in photographing the pretty wildflowers and wanted them properly identified.

All five of us kids loved Mom's homemade bread, and used to tease her to make it. It was half whole-wheat flour, half white, and sweetened with honey. She would let me stir the dough until it got too stiff for me, and then her strong arms would work more flour in until it was ready to knead. She made large batches, and moaned when they disappeared so fast, but as I grew up I recognized what all loving cooks know: That the appreciation of good food is much of the joy in the creation of it. It isn't worth making if it isn't eaten.

I confessed most of my wilder oat-sowings to Mom, and she didn't bat an eyelash. She calmly accepted the mishaps of my young adulthood. Most parents begin hinting when their daughters are in their 30s about marriage and grandchildren. Mom left me alone. If I didn't want to get married at all, that was fine with her, as long as I was happy. She thought every friend I introduced her to was "very nice." I'm absolutely sure she would have said that even if I had brought home unconventional partners. When I found Lance (actually, he found me, but that's another story) and married him, she took on an aura of deep contentment.

I miss Mom. I realize as I go through my days how many things I used to try to remember to tell her about. Last week in the garden, I was washing aphids off the Pak Chois with strong spray from the garden hose, and I wondered what Grandma Jessie used to do about aphids in her Massachusetts garden. "Mom could have told me," I thought, "But she's gone." With her is gone the inter-generational knowledge of her own mother as well.

The recipes which follow are for my Mom. She always liked it that I "took after" her. I hope she liked it too, that I did it in my own way. These recipes are mine, but she raised me to be what I am.

...from "Morning Hill News" #43, September/October '98

70

ADVANCED BAKING: YEASTED DOUGHS

Yeasted doughs are a little trickier to bake in a solar cooker. If they bake too slowly they may fall and turn out hard enough to use as paperweights! Use of an oven thermometer is very desirable here, so that you can tell how hot your solar cooker is getting. If it will not preheat to over 300 degrees, the sun is not intense enough or your cooker is not an efficient design for your area. If your cooker preheats to over 400 degrees, watch it carefully and prop the glass open a crack if it begins to get hot enough to smoke.

Baking only **one loaf at a time** allows your cooker to maintain a hotter temperature. Usually, when you put the loaf in, the temperature will drop below 300 degrees. Don't worry about this, it is normal. It is the mass of the loaf that causes the temperature to drop; and the temperature will climb back up some as the loaf cooks. By the time the loaf is done, the temperature will be up over 300 degrees, to a more normal baking temperature.

☼

If you have a nice clear sky and intense sun, you can increase the amount of dough you are baking by one-half, making an oval "peasant loaf" on a cookie sheet or in a shallow oval pan. These peasant loaves are attractive and have more crust per loaf, for your crust lovers.

Dark loaves bake faster and more efficiently than light ones, so this makes my favorite wholegrain breads also the best ones for solar baking. Try to use dark-coated baking pans, as they absorb more heat from the sun.

☼

Baking times vary, of course, depending on the intensity of your sun and the efficiency of your cooker. Still, once you become accustomed to cooking with the sun, you may be able to get a relative idea of the baking time from the "conventional kitchen" times given. Solar cooking times will usually be about 15 to 20 percent longer than conventional times for breads.

☼

When **baking these recipes in a conventional kitchen**, all recipes may be doubled (or increased by one-third, if a peasant loaf) to make two loaves.

BUTTERMILK BREAD

A large, tender, moist loaf.

Makes one 5X9-inch loaf:

  11/4 cups warm water
  2 teaspoons dry yeast
  Honey to proof
  2 tablespoons oil
  2 tablespoons honey
  1/2 teaspoon salt
  1/4 cup buttermilk powder
  3 to 4 cups whole wheat bread flour

   Put the warm water in a medium bread bowl, swirling it around to warm the bowl. Sprinkle the yeast over the water. Dip a clean spoon tip into your honey to get just a tiny bit, then stir into the yeast and water to dissolve it all together. Let rest in a warm place (called "proofing") until it foams up.
   Add the oil, honey and salt. Stir to combine well. In a small, dry bowl, mix the buttermilk powder with 1 cup of the flour. Beat into the yeast mixture. Continue adding flour to the dough 1/2 cup at a time, beating well with each addition, until too stiff to stir.
   Turn the dough out onto a floured board and knead until smooth and springy, about 7 minutes. Put the dough in a clean, oiled bowl, turning to oil the top. Cover and let rise in a warm place until double, about 11/2 hours.
   Set your solar cooker out to preheat.
   Form the dough into a loaf and place in an oiled 5X9-inch loaf pan. Let rise until double. Brush the top with a little water to make a crust.
   Bake in a preheated solar cooker until the loaf tests done (is crusty and brown on the top, and sounds hollow when tapped). Let rest in pan 5 minutes, then remove to a wire rack to cool.
   Because of the buttermilk in the dough, this will brown quickly. The loaf will be sticky and moist inside for a long time, and will probably need to bake a little longer than your usual bread.

❀

Conventional kitchen instructions: Bake loaves 40 to 45 minutes in a preheated 350-degree oven. If loaf browns too quickly, cover with a foil tent.

PAIN RUSTIQUE (RUSTIC BREAD)

A traditional bread and a nice combination of flavors. For full instructions on making and using sourdough starter, see the **Morning Hill Cookbook** (p.171).

Makes 1 oval peasant loaf:
11/3 cups warm water
2 teaspoons yeast
1 teaspoon honey
1 cup sourdough starter
2 tablespoons oil
2 tablespoons honey
1 teaspoon salt
2 tablespoons gluten flour (optional)
2 cups rye flour
2 cups whole wheat bread flour
Wheat flour to knead

In a large bread bowl, dissolve the yeast in the warm water with the teaspoon of honey. Allow to rest in a warm place 10 minutes until it foams up. Add the sourdough starter, oil, 2 tablespoons honey and salt. Stir well to combine. Add the gluten flour, if using, and 1 cup each of the rye and wheat flours. Beat well. Add rye and wheat flours in equal amounts until the dough is stiff enough to knead.

Knead 10 minutes, until the dough is very smooth and elastic. Place the dough in a clean, oiled bowl, and turn to oil the top. Cover and let rise until doubled, about 11/2 hours. Form into 1 oval loaf and place on a small, oiled cookie sheet (9X13-inch). Let rise until doubled, about 45 minutes.

Bake in a preheated solar cooker until the loaf tests done (sounds hollow when tapped on the bottom). Let rest in pan 5 minutes, then remove to a wire rack to cool. Cool thoroughly before storing.

❖

Conventional kitchen instructions: Bake loaves 35 to 40 minutes in a preheated 350-degree oven, or until the loaf tests done.

OATMEAL BREAD

This bread has a lovely texture and sweet flavor due to the oatmeal. If you want more tender oats, use hotter soaking water; for chewy oats, use cooler.

Makes 1 loaf:

> 1 cup old-fashioned rolled oats
> 1 cup hot tap water (120 to 130 degrees)
> 1/3 cup lukewarm water
> 2 teaspoons dry yeast
> 1 teaspoon honey
> 2 tablespoons oil
> 1 tablespoon honey
> 1 tablespoon molasses
> 1/2 teaspoon salt
> 1 tablespoon gluten flour (optional)
> About 3 cups whole wheat bread flour

In your bread bowl, stir together the oats and hot water. Let soak for 10 minutes.

In a 2-cup measure, dissolve the yeast and the teaspoon of honey in the 1/3 cup warm water. Let rest for 10 minutes or until it foams up.

Add the oil, honey, molasses and salt to the oat mixture. Stir in the proofed yeast. Mix the gluten flour with the first 2 cups of bread flour. Beat the flour well into the oat mixture until the dough begins to form strands. Add more bread flour 1/2 cup at a time until the dough becomes too stiff to stir.

Turn the dough out onto a floured board, and knead at least 7 minutes, adding more flour as needed to prevent sticking. This dough will remain just a little sticky. Place dough in an oiled bowl, turn to oil all sides; cover and let rise until double.

Set your solar cooker out to preheat. Turn dough out and form into a loaf. Place in an oiled 5X9-inch loaf pan and let rise until double. Bake in the preheated solar cooker until the loaf tests done. Let rest in pan 5 minutes, then remove to a wire rack to cool.

Conventional kitchen instructions: Bake loaves 35 to 40 minutes in a preheated 350-degree oven, or until the loaf tests done.

SOURDOUGH WHOLE WHEAT BREAD

A tasty, chewy loaf, somewhat larger than a standard loaf of bread. For full instructions on making and using sourdough starter, see the **Morning Hill Cookbook** (p.171).

Makes one peasant loaf:

> 1/4 cup warm water
> 2 teaspoons yeast
> 1 teaspoon honey
> 2 cups sourdough starter
> 3 to 4 cups whole wheat bread flour
> Coarse cornmeal

Dissolve the yeast and honey in the warm water and let rest in a warm place for about 10 minutes until it foams up (called "proofing" the yeast).

Add the starter to the proofed yeast. Add the first cup of bread flour and beat the dough well until it looks smooth and satiny and comes together in glutenous strands. Add more flour 1/2 cup at a time, beating well with each addition, until the dough is stiff enough to knead.

Turn the dough out onto a floured board and knead 8 to 10 minutes, until the dough springs back vigorously from an impression. Place the dough in an oiled bowl, turning once to oil the top. Cover and place in a warm spot to rise until doubled in bulk (about 1 to 11/2 hours). Prepare a cookie sheet or a pan at least 7X11-inch by oiling it and sprinkling it lightly with cornmeal. Punch the dough down and let rest a minute, then turn out of the bowl and form into 1 oblong loaf. Place the loaf on the prepared pan. Cover and let rise until doubled in bulk.

Brush the top of the loaf with a little water to make a crust. Bake in a preheated solar cooker until the loaf tests done. Cool the loaf thoroughly before storing in an airtight container.

⊕

Conventional kitchen instructions: Bake loaves 35 to 40 minutes in a preheated 350-degree oven, or until the loaf tests done.

POTATO-RYE ROLLS

Moist, chewy peasant rolls inspired by a Polish recipe.

Makes a 9X13-inch pan of 24 rolls:

- 11/4 cups warm water
- 1 tablespoon yeast
- 1 teaspoon honey
- 1 cup mashed potatoes
- 11/2 tablespoons dark molasses
- 1 tablespoon caraway seeds
- 1 teaspoon salt
- 2 tablespoons gluten flour
- 11/2 cups rye flour
- 2 to 3 cups whole wheat flour

In a medium-size bread bowl, dissolve the yeast with the honey in the warm water. Let rest in a warm place for 10 minutes. When the yeast foams up, add the mashed potatoes, molasses, caraway seed and salt. Stir well to blend. In a small bowl or cup, stir together the gluten flour and 1/2 cup of the rye flour. Beat into the yeast mixture. Then beat in 1/2 cup of the whole wheat flour, beating well till lumps are gone. Add rye and wheat flour in alternating 1/2 cups until the dough is too stiff to stir.

Turn the dough out onto a floured surface and knead with the whole wheat flour until springy and smooth, no less than 10 minutes. Place the dough in a clean, oiled bowl, turn to oil the top, and let rise in a warm place, covered, until double in bulk.

Set your solar cooker out to preheat. Prepare a 9X13-inch pan by oiling it lightly. When dough has doubled in bulk, turn it out on an oiled surface and form into rolls. Divide the dough into 24 equal pieces. Form into round rolls and place in prepared pan in 6 rows of 4 rolls each. Cover and let rise in a warm place until doubled in bulk. Brush the surface of the rolls lightly with a little water to make a crust. Bake in the preheated solar cooker until the rolls are brown on top, and test done. Serve hot, or cool completely before storing in an airtight container in a cool place.

✿

Conventional kitchen instructions: Bake in a preheated 350-degree oven for 30 to 35 minutes, or until they test done.

KAISER ROLLS

These rich rolls are glazed and sprinkled with sesame or poppy seeds for an elegant presentation.

Makes a 9X13-inch pan of 8 or 12 rolls:

 11/2 cups warm water
 1 tablespoon yeast
 2 tablespoons honey
 1 egg, beaten, divided
 2 tablespoons olive oil
 1/2 teaspoon salt
 3 to 4 cups whole wheat bread flour
 2 tablespoons gluten flour (optional)

In a large bowl, dissolve the yeast with the honey in the warm water. Let rest in a warm place for 10 minutes. When the yeast foams up, beat the egg in a small cup and pour most of it into the yeast, reserving about 1 tablespoon of it for the glaze. Put the reserved portion of the egg in the refrigerator.

Add the oil and salt to the yeast mixture, and beat in 2 cups of the whole wheat flour and the gluten flour if using. Continue beating vigorously until gluten strands form. Add more whole wheat flour until dough becomes too stiff to stir.

Turn the dough out onto a floured board, and knead 8 to 10 minutes until smooth and very springy. Place the dough in a clean, oiled bowl, turning to oil the top. Cover and let rise in a warm place until double in bulk, about 11/2 hours. Punch down, form into rolls as follows:

Decide if you want 8 large rolls, or 12 somewhat smaller ones. Oil the 9X13-inch pan lightly. Divide the dough and roll each piece into a rope about 8 inches long. Twist the rope at the center, and wrap the ends so the center pokes up. Pinch the outside end to the body of the roll. Place in the pan, 4 rows long by 2 or 3 rows wide. Pat the rolls into place.

Set your solar cooker out to preheat. Let the rolls rise until double in bulk, about 45 minutes. Dilute the reserved egg with an equal amount of water, and brush it over the tops of the rolls with a pastry brush. Sprinkle poppy seeds or sesame seeds lightly over the glaze.

Bake in the preheated solar cooker until the tops of the rolls are golden and the rolls test done. Cool in pan 10 minutes, then remove and serve, or cool thoroughly on rack before storing.

Conventional kitchen instructions: Bake in a preheated 350-degree oven for 30 to 35 minutes, until tops are golden and rolls test done.

ONION-HERB ROLLS

Flavorful rolls to serve with a simple soup meal or to make a whole lunch with the addition of a little cheese or spread.

Makes a 9X13-inch pan of 15 or 24 rolls:

    1 tablespoon yeast
    11/2 cups warm water
    3 tablespoons honey
    2 tablespoons olive oil
    1 teaspoon salt
    1 cup finely chopped onion
    1 teaspoon dried basil, crushed
    1 teaspoon dried rosemary, crushed
    4 to 5 cups whole wheat bread flour

In a large bowl, dissolve the yeast with the honey in the warm water. Let rest 10 minutes. Add the oil, salt, chopped onion and herbs to the yeast mixture, and beat in 2 cups of the whole wheat flour. Continue beating vigorously until gluten strands form. Add more whole wheat flour until dough becomes too stiff to stir.

Turn the dough out onto a floured board, and knead 8 to 10 minutes until smooth and very springy. The bits of onion may fall out as you knead, but just keep putting them back on the dough and folding it over them. Place the dough in a clean, oiled bowl, turning to oil the top. Cover and let rise in a warm place until double in bulk, about 11/2 hours.

Put your solar cooker out to preheat. Oil a 9X13-inch baking pan, and set it near your work surface. Turn the dough out onto the surface and divide and form 24 rolls as in the recipe above. Make 6 rows of 4 rolls. Cover the pan and put in a warm place.

Let rise until double in bulk, about 45 minutes. Brush the tops gently with a little water. Bake in the preheated solar cooker until the tops of the rolls are golden and the rolls test done. Cool in pan 10 minutes, then remove and serve, or cool thoroughly on rack before storing.

Conventional kitchen instructions: Bake in a preheated 350-degree oven for 30 to 35 minutes, until tops are golden and rolls test done.

MULTI-GRAIN ROLLS

These chewy rolls accompany a hearty dinner or soup.

Makes a 9X13-inch pan of 24 rolls:

11/4 cups rolled multi-grain cereal
2 cups warm water
1 tablespoon yeast
3/4 cup lukewarm water
1 teaspoon honey
1/2 teaspoon salt
2 tablespoons honey
3 tablespoons oil
4 to 5 cups whole wheat bread flour
2 tablespoons gluten flour (optional)

In a small saucepan, combine the cereal and the 2 cups of water. Bring to a simmer and cook for 5 minutes, stirring frequently. Remove from heat and scrape into a large bowl. Add the salt, 2 tablespoons honey, and oil to the cereal, then cool the mixture to lukewarm.

Dissolve the yeast in the 3/4 cup of water with the 1 teaspoon honey. Let rest 10 minutes in a warm place. When the yeast foams up, combine it with the cereal mixture. Beat in 2 cups of the bread flour, and the gluten flour if using (it will make the rolls lighter, but it is a refined product). Beat well until gluten strands form between the spoon and the bowl. Add more bread flour, 1/2 cup at a time, until the dough is stiff enough to knead.

Knead the dough on a floured surface at least 7 minutes, until it is smooth and springy. Place the dough in a clean oiled bowl, turn and cover it, and let rise in a warm place until double in bulk, about 11/2 hours.

Set your solar cooker out to preheat. Oil a 9X13-inch baking pan, and set it near your work surface. Turn the dough out onto the surface and divide into 24 equal portions. Form them into rolls as follows: flatten each piece between your palms and work the air out of it. Fold and roll it and shape it into a ball, then place it smooth side up in the pan. Make 6 rows of 4 rolls. Cover the pan and put in a warm place to rise until double.

Bake in the preheated solar cooker until the tops of the rolls are golden and the rolls test done. Cool in pan 10 minutes, then remove and serve warm, or cool thoroughly on rack before storing.

Conventional kitchen instructions: Bake in a preheated 375-degree oven for 25 to 30 minutes, until tops are golden and rolls test done.

HOLIDAY ROLLS

The warm golden color and flecks of spice in these rolls make them perfect for a holiday meal.

Makes a 9X13-inch pan of a dozen rolls:

    11/2 cups warm water
    Pinch of saffron strands
    6 cardamom pods
    1 tablespoon yeast
    3 tablespoons honey
    1/2 teaspoon salt
    1 egg
    2 tablespoons oil
    2/3 cup raisins
    1/3 cup non-instant milk powder
    2 tablespoons gluten flour (optional)
    4 to 5 cups fine whole wheat bread flour

Put the warm water into a large mixing bowl, and crush the saffron strands into it. Break open the cardamom pods and take out the seeds. Crush the seeds lightly in a mortar and pestle, and add to the water. Allow to steep 5 minutes. Add the yeast and honey. Let the mixture rest 10 minutes in a warm place, until the yeast foams up.

Add the egg, oil, and raisins. In a separate small bowl, stir the milk powder and gluten flour into the first cup of bread flour. Beat the flour into the liquid, adding more and beating well with each addition until the dough is stiff enough to knead.

Knead the dough 5 to 7 minutes, or until very smooth and springy. Place in an oiled bowl, turning to oil top. Cover and let rise till double, about 11/2 hours.

Set your solar cooker out to preheat. Knead the dough again, and shape into 12 rolls. Place the rolls in an oiled 9X13-inch pan, cover, and let rise till double.

Bake in the preheated solar cooker until the tops of the rolls are golden and the rolls test done. Cool in pan 10 minutes, then remove and serve warm, or cool thoroughly on rack before storing.

⊕

Conventional kitchen instructions: Bake in a preheated 350-degree oven for 25 to 30 minutes, until tops are golden and rolls test done.

ORANGE-POPPYSEED BREAKFAST ROLLS

These rolls need no adornment, but a little raspberry jam will elevate them to the sublime! Please use organic oranges, because you will be using the peel.

Makes a 9X13-inch pan of 24 rolls:

    2 large oranges
    1/4 cup finely chopped date pieces
    3 tablespoons honey
    2 tablespoons poppy seeds
    1 tablespoon dry yeast
    1/2 teaspoon salt
    2 tablespoons oil
    4 to 5 cups fine whole wheat bread flour

Get out a medium bread bowl. Using the fine side of the grater, grate the orange part of the peel off the two oranges. Squeeze the juice from the oranges, and add enough warm water to make 2 cups of liquid. Add the liquid to the peel in the bowl.

Add the chopped dates, honey and poppy seed. Stir well to combine. Sprinkle the yeast over the mixture, and stir to dissolve. Let rest in a warm place for 10 minutes, or until the yeast foams up.

Add the salt and oil, then stir in the flour until stiff enough to knead. Turn the dough out onto a floured board, and knead at least 7 minutes, or until smooth and springy. Place the dough in an oiled bowl, turning to oil the top, cover, and let rise 2 hours or until doubled in bulk.

Set your solar cooker out to preheat. Prepare a 9X13-inch pan by oiling it lightly. Divide the dough into 24 equal pieces, and shape the pieces into round rolls. Arrange in the pan in 6 rows of 4 rolls. Cover and let rise about 45 minutes, until double.

Bake in the preheated solar cooker until the tops of the rolls are golden and the rolls test done. Cool in pan 10 minutes, then remove and serve warm, or cool thoroughly on rack before storing. If these rolls will be kept more than a day, they are best kept in the refrigerator.

Conventional kitchen instructions: Bake in a preheated 350-degree oven for 25 to 30 minutes, until tops are golden and rolls test done.

PRUNE-DATE RING

This is a classic sweet breakfast pastry, with a thick, fruity filling.

Makes a 9X13-inch pastry ring:

> 1 cup warm water
> 2 tablespoons dry milk powder
> 3 tablespoons oil
> 3 tablespoons honey
> 2 teaspoons dry yeast
> 1 egg
> 1/2 teaspoon salt
> 3 cups fine whole wheat flour (high gluten, or if using pastry flour
>   add 1 tablespoon gluten flour per cup)
> **Prune-date Filling** (on next page)
> About 1/4 cup broken nut meats (optional)

Make the fruit filling the afternoon before making the dough.

In a medium-large bowl, whisk the milk powder into the warm water. Whisk in the oil and honey. Dissolve the yeast into the mixture, add the egg, and mix well. Allow to rest in a warm place for about 10 minutes, or until the mixture begins to foam up. Add 2 cups of the flour and beat well. Continue stirring in flour until the dough forms a ball.

Turn the dough out onto a floured board and knead at least 5 minutes, until springy and smooth. Put the dough back in a clean, oiled bowl, cover and let rise 1 hour.

Turn the dough out onto a floured board, and roll out to an oblong about 10X20-inch. Spread the filling lengthwise down the middle third. Sprinkle with nuts if desired. Fold the two long edges over the filling. Roll onto an oiled 9X13 baking sheet with the double layer down. Bring the two ends of the roll around to form an oval, and pinch the ends together.

With a sharp knife, make cuts about 1 inch apart all the way around through the top layer of dough. Put a hand through the center of the roll, and one on the outside. Gently lifting and stretching, pull the dough towards all the corners of the sheet. The bottom layers will stretch, and the top one will part to show the filling.

Put your solar cooker out to preheat. Cover the ring with a clean tea-towel and let rise until nearly double in bulk, about 45 minutes. When the ring is risen, brush a little water over the top strips of dough to make a glaze. Bake in the preheated solar cooker until the crust on top is golden, and the dough tests done. Let rest on pan for 5 minutes, then use a spatula to slide off onto a rack to cool.

This is delicious warm, and will keep for a few days at room temperature.

PRUNE-DATE FILLING

3/4 cup chopped dates
3/4 cup chopped prunes
3/4 cup boiling water
1 tablespoon honey
1/4 teaspoon almond extract

Soak the fruit overnight with the hot water and honey. In the morning, stir in the almond extract, beating well until the filling is thick.

Conventional kitchen instructions: Increase the hot water in the filling to 1 cup. In the morning, if the fruit has not soaked up all the water, cook over low heat, stirring frequently, until thick. Add the almond extract, then cool until lukewarm.

Bake the ring in a preheated 350-degree oven for about 25 minutes, or until the top is golden and the ring is done.

CINNAMON-OAT ROLLS

Chewy, nutty, spicy and delicious! These rolls take a little extra time, but they are worth every minute.

Makes a 9X13 pan of 24 rolls:

1 1/2 cups rolled oats
2 cups warm water
1 tablespoon yeast
1/2 cup lukewarm water
1 teaspoon honey
1/2 teaspoon salt
3 tablespoons oil
1/4 cup honey
2 tablespoons gluten flour
4 to 5 cups bread flour

Filling:
4 tablespoons honey
1 teaspoon brown rice flour
4 teaspoons cinnamon
1/3 cup broken walnuts
3/4 cup raisins

Combine the oats and the 2 cups of water. Let soak for 10 minutes. Meanwhile, proof the yeast in the 1/2 cup of water with the 1 teaspoon honey. When the yeast foams up, combine the two mixtures and add the salt, 2 tablespoons honey, and oil.

Beat in the gluten flour and 2 cups of the bread flour. Beat well until gluten strands form between the spoon and the bowl. Add more bread flour, 1/2 cup at a time, until the dough is ready to knead.

Knead the dough on a floured surface at least 7 minutes, until it is smooth and springy. Place the dough in a clean oiled bowl, cover it, and let rise in a warm place until double in bulk. Warm the honey in your solar cooker just till it is liquid, and stir in the rice flour and cinnamon. Have the nuts and raisins handy.

Preheat your solar cooker. Oil a 9X13-inch baking pan, and set it near your work surface. Turn the dough out onto the surface and roll out to a 1X2- foot oblong. Spread the cinnamon mixture on the dough, and sprinkle evenly with the nuts and raisins. Roll across the short direction, so you have a "log" about 24 inches long.

Cut the log into 24 equal, about 1-inch slices. Place the slices in the pan, cut side up. Make 6 rows of 4 rolls. Cover the pan and put in a warm place to rise until double. Bake in the preheated solar cooker until the tops of the rolls are golden and the rolls test done. Cool in pan 10 minutes, then remove and serve warm or cool on rack before storing.

Conventional kitchen instructions: Bake in a preheated 375-degree oven for 25 to 30 minutes, until tops are golden and rolls test done.

RHUBARB ROLY-POLY

Great for breakfast, snacking, or a not-too-sweet dessert.

Makes a 5X9-inch loaf:
Dough: 1 cup warm water
        1 tablespoon yeast
        1 teaspoon honey
        1 egg
        1/2 teaspoon salt
        1/4 cup oil
        1/3 cup honey
        1/4 cup milk powder
        2 tablespoons soy flour
        1 tablespoon gluten flour (optional)
        3 to 4 cups bread flour
Filling: 1/4 cup honey
        2 cups diced rhubarb (1/4 to 1/2-inch)

In a large bowl, proof the yeast with the honey in the warm water. When the yeast foams, add the egg, salt, oil, and honey. Mix together the milk powder, soy flour, gluten flour, and first 2 cups of bread flour. Add to the yeast mixture, and beat well until strands of gluten form. Add enough more bread flour to make a stiff dough. Cover and let rise for 30 minutes while you dice the rhubarb.

Dice the rhubarb into 1/4 to 1/2-inch pieces. Don't worry about making it regular. Pour the honey over it and stir. Set aside.

Lightly oil a 5X9-inch loaf pan. Set aside. Turn the dough out onto a floured board and knead until smooth and springy, 5 to 7 minutes. Roll out to a 9X15-inch oblong. Spread the rhubarb openly over the dough oblong, with its juice. Starting with a short edge, roll the dough up into a 9-inch long loaf. Place the loaf in the pan.

Set your solar cooker out to preheat. Let the loaf rise until increased in bulk by 50 percent. Bake in the preheated cooker until the loaf is golden on top and tests done. Let rest in pan 5 minutes, then loosen around sides and remove to rack. Slice like bread, and serve warm or at room temperature.

Conventional kitchen instructions: Bake in a preheated 350-degree oven for 40 to 50 minutes.

HONEY TWIRLS

When I was in college, the cafeteria called these "Cinnamon Knots" and I was addicted to them! Some people also call them "Sticky Buns."

Makes 1 dozen:
- 2/3 cup warm water
- 2 teaspoons dry yeast
- 2 tablespoons oil
- 2 tablespoons honey
- 1/4 teaspoon salt
- 1 egg
- 3 tablespoons milk powder
- 2 cups fine whole wheat bread flour

Filling:
- 2 tablespoons oil
- 1/4 cup honey
- 1 teaspoon cinnamon
- 1/2 cup broken pecans or walnuts

In a large bowl or small bread bowl, dissolve the yeast into the warm water. Add the oil and honey, and let rest in a warm place for 10 minutes, or until the yeast foams up. Add the salt and egg, and beat well. Stir the milk powder into the flour, and add to the liquid in the bowl. Beat well until gluten strands form.

Warm the oil, honey, and cinnamon for the filling together just until they will blend easily. Roll out the dough on a well-floured board to a 12-inch square. Spread half of the filling on it, and sprinkle with half of the nuts. Roll up, and cut across the log with a sharp knife to make 12 equal pieces.

Oil a 12-section muffin tin. Combine the remaining filling and nuts, and divide evenly among the tins. Place rolls, cut side down, in the tins. Cover and let rise in a warm place until double, about 1 hour. Meanwhile, set your solar cooker out to preheat.

Bake the rolls in solar cooker until the tops are golden-brown and they test done. Remove from pan immediately by twisting each roll as you lift it out. Invert on rack and cool sticky-side up. Best eaten warm!

☼

Conventional kitchen instructions: Bake in a preheated 350-degree oven for 20 to 25 minutes, until golden and crusty on top.

Cookies

THE ZEN OF FOOD PRESERVATION

I've spent large portions of the last several weekends squirreling food away for the winter. In the cool of the morning, Lance goes out to the garden and returns with giant bowls of Pak Choi plants. He brings in cauliflowers as big as a basketball, heaps of green broccoli shoots, sliding piles of snap peas. Within a few hours the untidy heaps are reduced to freezer bags packed full.

When the morning sun dries the dew off the leaves, I take my orange-handled scissors and go out to the garden to gather herbs for drying. In the house, it doesn't take long to tie and hang them on the rack above the wood cookstove. In a week I will have sage, oregano, lemon thyme and savory leaves ready to pack away in airtight containers in a cool, dark corner.

The afternoon sun warms the berries and intensifies their flavor. When I uncover the strawberry bed, the aroma of the ripe fruit envelops me. I dodge hungry yellowjackets to get my share, but I don't mind them as much since Lance told me they also eat those little green worms that like our cauliflower. My share of the strawberries and raspberries will be turned into sauce for winter desserts, just crushed raw berries sweetened with a dab of honey.

The gooseberries aren't sweet or tender enough to use raw, and the bushes have produced a couple of gallons of them this year, so I spend part of an afternoon "tipping and tailing" them, pinching off the stem and blossom ends. I put my chair outside our back door and set a bowl full of washed berries on a crate in front of me. In the shade of the pine trees, with woodpeckers and chickadees frequenting our feeders 20 feet away, the time passes quickly, and soon bowls of berries await morning, and jam, in the refrigerator.

It's Lance's success in the garden which allows me to have all this bounty to preserve. When he first came here, people told him he couldn't grow anything in this climate with its average 16-day season between 32-degree nights. A few tenacious gardeners in Seneca, across the valley, were quietly growing green things in spite of the extension agent's predictions. No one was as determined as Lance. When one method failed, he would invent and try another, and another, until he had figured out how to grow so many different things that we had more than we could possibly eat during the summers.

Of course, growing more than we could eat was the whole idea. The idea is to grow enough so that we can put food by and eat the bounty of our garden year round, even when the scene inside the deer fence is of snow dimpled over empty boxed beds and bare brambles. We go to the root cellar and heap a bowl with potatoes and carrots. We go to the freezer and sort over vegetables, and add a packet of strawberries for a treat. In the corner of the bedroom hang bags of garlic and onions. On a shelf are jars of rich fruit chutney. We'll have curried vegetables for dinner, with a winter cabbage salad and strawberry sundaes for dessert.

"Fresh" peaches from Chile on the grocery store display in January? None for me, thanks. I've got summer in a jar.

...from "Morning Hill News" #37, September/October '97

CHERRY CAKES

These delicate morsels are bejeweled with bright, tart dried cherry bits. If you cannot find dried cherries, use any other dried fruit (prunes, raisins) cut in small pieces.

Makes about 21/2 dozen:

    1/4 cup oil
    1/4 cup honey
    2 eggs
    1/2 teaspoon dried orange peel
    3/4 cup plus 2 tablespoons whole wheat pastry flour
    1/3 cup dried cherries, cut into small pieces
    1/3 cup hazelnuts, chopped
    1/4 cup finely chopped dried apricots

Set your solar cooker out to preheat, and lightly oil a cookie sheet.

In a medium bowl, beat together the oil, honey, eggs, and orange peel. Add the flour, fruit, and nuts. Mix well to blend. The dough will be very soft.

Drop by teaspoonfuls on the cookie sheets. The cookies will spread as they bake, but not too much. Bake in the solar cooker just until the cookies turn golden at the edges and are well set up in the centers.

Remove the cookies to a rack to cool, and store in an airtight container in a cool place.

Conventional kitchen instructions: Bake in a preheated 350-degree oven for 12 to 15 minutes.

APPLE-OAT-NUT BARS

Chewy, nutty, tender & moist. Use a type of apple like Jonathan or MacIntosh that cooks up tender and soft.

Makes an 8X8-inch pan of 16 bars:

   1 cup diced apple (1/4-inch)
   1 tablespoon water
   2 tablespoons honey
   1/2 teaspoon cinnamon
   1 teaspoon fresh lemon juice
   1/4 cup honey
   1/4 cup oil
   1 egg
   1/2 cup whole wheat pastry flour
   11/4 cups rolled oats
   1 teaspoon baking powder
   1/2 cup broken walnuts

Set your solar cooker out to preheat. Prepare an 8X8-inch square baking pan by oiling it lightly and lining it with baker's paper if desired.

In a jar in the cooker, steam the diced apple, water, 2 tablespoons honey, and cinnamon together until the apple is tender and the juice is thickened to the consistency of honey.

Cool the apple mixture to lukewarm, then add the lemon juice, 1/4 cup honey, oil, and egg. Beat well to mix. In a separate bowl, stir together the flour, oats, baking powder and nuts. Add to the apple mixture, and stir to blend. Scrape into the prepared pan, and spread evenly.

Bake in the preheated cooker until the cake is golden and springy to the touch. Remove to a rack to cool. When cool, cut into 16 bars with a long, serrated knife.

When completely cool, store in an airtight container in a cool place.

⊕

Conventional kitchen instructions: Steam the apple, water and honey in a small saucepan over medium-low heat, being careful that it does not dry out and adding more water if necessary. Bake in a preheated 350-degree oven for 30 minutes, until the cake tests done.

FRUIT-OAT COOKIE BARS

A dried fruit and nut combo makes a great snacking bar. Use whatever fruits you have on hand, or a combination.

Makes a 7X11-inch pan of 24 cookies:

1/4 cup raisins
1/4 cup dried cherries, apricots, or pineapple
Hot water to soak fruit
1 cup whole wheat pastry flour
1 1/4 cups rolled oats
1/2 teaspoon baking soda
1/2 teaspoon baking powder
1/4 cup chopped walnuts
1/4 cup oil
2/3 cup honey
1 egg
2 tablespoons water (use soaking water from fruit)

Set your solar cooker out to preheat. Prepare a 7X11-inch brownie pan by oiling it lightly.

Soak any of your fruits that are not fresh and plump in a little hot water for 5 minutes (otherwise, they will extract moisture from the cookies after baking, making them go stale faster). Meanwhile, in a medium bowl, stir together the flour, oats, soda and baking powder. Drain the fruits and save the water. Chop the fruits to raisin-sized bits. Toss the raisins, fruits and nuts in the flour mixture to coat. Set aside.

Mix the oil, honey, egg, and 2 tablespoons soaking water. Stir in the dry mixture with the fruits. Scrape the batter into the prepared pan, and bake in the solar cooker until the top is golden and the cake tests done.

Remove the pan to a rack, and allow to cool for 10 minutes before removing the cake. Cool completely before cutting. Cut into 24 bars.

Conventional kitchen instructions: Bake in a preheated 350-degree oven for 25 to 30 minutes, or until the cake tests done.

DATE SPICE BARS

These cookies can be kept in airtight tins for up to two weeks.

Makes one 7X11-inch pan of 18 cookie bars:

2 eggs
1/2 cup honey
1 teaspoon freshly grated orange peel, or 1/2 teaspoon dried
1 cup whole wheat pastry flour
1 teaspoon baking powder
1/4 teaspoon ground allspice
1 cup chopped dates
3/4 cup broken walnuts

Set your solar cooker out to preheat. Prepare a 7X11-inch cake pan by oiling it and lining it with baker's paper, if desired.

Beat eggs until thick, then beat in honey and orange peel. Sift the flour, baking powder and allspice together and stir in. Add dates and nuts, and combine all ingredients thoroughly. Spread the mixture in the prepared pan, and bake in the preheated solar cooker until dark golden and springy to the touch.

Remove from pan and cool on a wire rack. With a long, serrated knife, cut into 18 bars. Store in airtight tins.

Conventional kitchen instructions: Bake in a preheated 350-degree oven for 30 to 35 minutes.

CHOCOLATE-APPLESAUCE BROWNIES

You can't really get fudgy brownies without hardened fats, but these are pretty close!

Makes a 7X11-inch pan of 12 brownies:

> 1 cup whole wheat pastry flour
> 1/2 cup unsweetened cocoa powder
> 1/2 teaspoon baking powder
> 1/4 teaspoon baking soda
> 1/4 cup oil
> 2/3 cup honey
> 3/4 cup strained applesauce
> 2 eggs
> 1 teaspoon vanilla extract
> 1/2 cup coarsely chopped walnuts (optional)

Set your solar cooker out to preheat. Lightly oil a 7X11-inch brownie pan.

Sift together the pastry flour, cocoa powder, baking powder and soda. Set aside. In a medium bowl, beat the oil, honey, applesauce, eggs and vanilla extract vigorously with a spoon until well-mixed. Stir in the flour mixture. Fold in the nuts, if using.

Spread the mixture in the prepared pan. Bake in solar cooker until the brownies test done. Cool in pan 10 minutes, then cut into 12 brownies and remove to rack with a spatula. Cool thoroughly before storing in an airtight container in a cool place.

☼

Conventional kitchen instructions: Bake in a preheated 350-degree oven for 25 to 30 minutes.

JAM BARS

This is a wonderfully healthy version of those chewy, sweet confections.

Makes an 8X8-inch pan of 16 bars:
Crust: 1/4 cup honey
2 tablespoons oil
1/2 teaspoon vanilla
1 cup rolled oats
1/2 cup walnuts
1 egg
2 tablespoons honey
1/4 cup whole wheat pastry flour
1/2 teaspoon baking powder
1/2 cup thick homemade jam

Filling: 1 egg, beaten
1/4 cup honey
2 tablespoons whole wheat pastry flour
1/4 teaspoon baking powder
2 teaspoons lemon juice
1/3 cup unsweetened coconut flakes

Set your solar cooker out to preheat. Line an 8X8-inch cake pan with bakers paper.

Have the 2 tablespoons honey, oil and vanilla at room temperature or warmer. Stir to blend well. Add the oats, and toss to coat with the honey mixture. Let soak for 5 minutes. Add the walnuts.

Beat the egg, honey, flour, and baking powder together until frothy. Stir into the oat mixture. Spread the dough in the prepared pan, and bake about 15 minutes, or until set and just beginning to color on top.

Meanwhile, make the filling (you can use the same bowl). To the beaten egg, add the pastry flour, baking powder, lemon juice and coconut. Beat until frothy.

When the crust is beginning to color, remove it from the cooker. Spread it with the jam, and pour the filling carefully over the top. Return it to the cooker, and continue baking until the crust is golden and set, about 15 minutes more. Remove, and cool 5 minutes.

Use the paper to pull the cake from the pan. You will probably have to use a knife around the edges to separate the paper from the filling. Cool the cake completely before cutting into 16 bars. Store in a cool place.

Conventional kitchen instructions: Bake in a preheated 350-degree oven. Crust may take 20 minutes to bake, filling will probably take 15.

HAZELNUT BROWNIES

These simple brownies are very elegant! Don't overlook the possibility of serving them with fruit and ice cream for dessert.

Makes an 8X8-inch pan of 9 brownies:

> 1/2 cup hazelnuts
> 2/3 cup honey
> 2 eggs
> 1/2 teaspoon vanilla
> 2/3 cup whole wheat pastry flour
> 1/2 teaspoon baking powder

Set your solar cooker out to preheat. Oil an 8X8-inch pan and line it with baker's paper if desired.

Grind the hazelnuts in a blender until they resemble coarse flour. It is not necessary to remove the skins, but if you wish to do so, you may toast the hazelnuts in the solar cooker until the skins crack, then cool and rub the skins off.

Beat the hazelnuts in a medium bowl with the honey, eggs, and vanilla. Stir the flour and baking powder together in a cup, and then add them to the nut mixture. Scrape the batter into the prepared pan.

Bake in the preheated solar cooker for 35 minutes, or until the mixture sets up. Let cool in the pan for 10 minutes. Use an oiled spatula to cut and remove the brownies to a rack to cool completely.

Conventional kitchen instructions: Skins may be removed from the nuts by toasting them for 10 minutes in a 350-degree oven, then following instructions above. Bake the brownies in a preheated 325-degree oven for 35 minutes, or until the mixture sets up.

APPLE-NUT SQUARES

These goodies will definitely satisfy a sweet tooth! Meringue-topped squares of apple cake.

Makes a 9X13 pan of 24 squares:

    3 tablespoons oil
    1/2 cup honey
    1 tablespoon molasses
    3 egg yolks
    1/2 teaspoon vanilla
    11/2 cups whole wheat pastry flour
    1 teaspoon baking powder
    11/4 cups apple, peeled and chopped
    3 egg whites
    1/2 cup honey
    1/2 teaspoon vanilla
    1/3 cup chopped walnuts

Set your solar cooker out to preheat. Oil a 9X13-inch pan and line it with baker's paper.

In a medium bowl, beat the oil, honey, molasses, egg yolks, and vanilla with a spoon until well-blended. Sift the flour and baking powder together into another bowl, and toss the chopped apple with the flour mixture. Combine the two mixtures, and spread in the prepared pan. Bake in the preheated solar cooker just until the mixture is set and beginning to turn light golden on top.

Meanwhile, prepare the meringue. The egg whites and honey should be at room temperature. Beat the egg whites until stiff peaks form. Drizzle in the honey, beating constantly, until it is incorporated. Add the vanilla, and beat to combine. Remove the cake from the cooker and spread the meringue over it. Sprinkle the chopped nuts over the meringue. Return to the solar cooker and bake until the meringue has set and turned golden on top.

Cool 10 minutes in pan, then use the paper liner to pull the cake out of the pan and slide it onto a rack to cool thoroughly. Use care to separate the paper from the meringue. When cool, slide the cake onto a cutting board. Cut with a sharp knife into 24 squares, and use a spatula to remove the squares from the paper. Store in a single layer in an airtight container.

Conventional kitchen instructions: Bake the dough 10 to 12 minutes in a preheated 350-degree oven, until beginning to set up. Bake with the meringue about 10 to 12 minutes more at 350 degrees, or until set and beginning to turn golden on top.

Sources

Solar Cookers International
-- nonprofit promoting solar cooking worldwide
1919 21st Street #101
Sacramento, CA 95811
916-455-4499
http://solarcookers.org/

Jennifer's Solar Cooking Page:
-- my favorite links and solar cooking events
http://home.centurytel.net/morninghill/solarcook.htm

The Solar Cooking Wiki
-- links to all things solar cooking
http://solarcooking.wikia.com

Sun Ovens International, Inc.
-- The Sun Oven
39W835 Midan Drive
Elburn, IL 60119
1-800-408-7919
sunovens@execpc.com
http://www.sunoven.com/

Heaven's Flame, A Guide to
Solar Cookers
by Joseph Radabaugh
Home Power Publishing
P.O. Box 275
Ashland, OR 97520
800-707-6585

Solar Energy International
P.O. Box 715
Carbondale, CO 81623
970-963-8855
sei@solarenergy.org
www.solarenergy.org

Suntoys
-- solar bubblepack cooker
David Piper
PO Box 622
Renton, WA 98057
206-230-5286
www.solar-slow-cooker.com

Solar Box Cookers Northwest
7036 18th Ave. N.E.
Seattle, WA 98115

Index

99

Praise for "The Morning Hill Cookbook"

"I've been using a friend's cookbook and I haven't wanted to give it back. I've been looking for this book forever! Thanks." Jani Whitacre, Rhododendron, Oregon.

"I gave a copy to my girlfriend at work and she got nothing constructive done for the rest of the day -- she couldn't put it down!" Miriam Fauteck, Chicago, Illinois.

"Barker's recipes reflect her eating-in-harmony-with-the-season philosophy. ...There's an endearingly personal feel to Barker's work. ....Morning Hill serves up a liberal helping of tips for the chef. ...This isn't haute cuisine. Barker emphasizes ingredients that for the most part are readily available and easy to find. ...Barker's recipes appeal to the eye as well as the taste buds." Suzanne Johnson in **The Capital Press Agriculture Weekly**, Salem, Oregon.

"As a source of flavorful, easy to prepare recipes that are in tune with the seasons and the spirit of the gardener...I highly recommend **The Morning Hill Cookbook**." Sandra Kocher in **The Natural Farmer**.

"Her vegetarian recipes reflect the earnest, thoughtful way she and her husband, Lance, cheerfully approach self-sufficiency in a demanding environment." Bethanye McNichol in **The Good Heart Cooking School Newsletter**.

"This woman really knows how to cook!" Kathleen Jarschke-Schultze, **Home Power Magazine**.

"I first met Jennifer at one of her cooking classes. I was concerned about eating healthier, more natural foods. I have kept coming back because of the great food, and Jennifer's enthusiastic concern for others and our environment. Her recipes are easy to follow, always turn out perfect, and are delicious!" Cindy Waldo, cooking class student.

"The recipes...are scrumptious!" Richard Richardson, Deering, Alaska.

The Morning Hill Solar Cookery Book contains more prize-winning recipes from the solar homestead in eastern Oregon where Jennifer and Lance Barker live. Jennifer has been cooking professionally for 10 years, and cooking with the sun for the last five. "The sun calls out the creativity in me! I have to cook new things! I can't stop!"

order form

Name _____

Address _____

_____

The Morning Hill Solar Cookery Book
Number of copies _____   x $14.95 each   = total   _____

The Morning Hill Cookbook
Number of copies _____   x $13.95 each   = total   _____

(no extra charge for postage)   Total enclosed   _____

Send to: Jennifer Stein Barker
          Morning Hill Associates
          15013 Geary Cr Rd
          Canyon City, OR 97820

Make check payable to: Jennifer Stein Barker.
Write for volume pricing for co-ops, groups and stores.

----

order form

Name _____

Address _____

_____

The Morning Hill Solar Cookery Book
Number of copies _____   x $14.95 each   = total   _____

The Morning Hill Cookbook
Number of copies _____   x $13.95 each   = total   _____

(no extra charge for postage)   Total enclosed   _____

Send to: Jennifer Stein Barker
          Morning Hill Associates
          15013 Geary Cr Rd
          Canyon City, OR 97820

Make check payable to: Jennifer Stein Barker.
Write for volume pricing for co-ops, groups and stores.